Jesus Christ
Our Intelligent Designer

An Evaluation of
The Intelligent Design Movement

Revised Edition

John C. Whitcomb

"Whoever is ashamed of Me and My words,
the Son of Man will be ashamed of him
when He comes in His glory"
(Luke 9:26)

JESUS CHRIST: OUR INTELLIGENT DESIGNER
Revised Edition

Kainos Books
Waxhaw, North Carolina
kainosbooks.com

ISBN – 13: 978-0615609461

Special thanks to Mrs. Vickie J. Broyles for preparing the indexes.

Visit Whitcomb Ministries on the Web at
www.whitcombministries.org

Contents

Foreword

John Morris

Life's amazing complexity cannot be denied. We see all around us a seeming universality of perfection. The inner complexity of living creatures is matched by well-planned symbiotic relationships between life-forms, a mutual dependency that defies claims of a sequential appearance of the entities involved. Nature has balance, from the intricate food chain to a recycling of resources. The plant and animal kingdoms give every appearance of having been created, on purpose, by a very wise Creator. Christians give Him great glory for His creative power and planning.

Evolutionists see the same universality of perfection, yet they deny any creative agent and ascribe it to unthinking, impersonal natural causes. The irreducible complexity of life, which seems obvious to anyone who believes in the existence of a supernatural Creator, is ascribed by evolutionary scientists to mindless natural selection.

How can evolutionists do this? Is it logical? Is it credible? What is the thought system that permits such a conclusion? First and foremost is a faith commitment to naturalism, an interpretive system in which natural causes are the only ones allowed. Some adherents have even gone so far as to redefine "science" as "naturalism." Instead of science being the search for truth, it has become the search for a believable naturalistic explanation for every scientific observation. Natural selection becomes a God substitute, seemingly omnipresent, omniscient, and omnipotent. "It" can accomplish anything and has accomplished everything. No supernatural agency has ever been involved.

Some naturalists would insist that even if creation by a Creator is true, it cannot form the basis for a valid scientific approach. Strict naturalism is required by science, they say. This commitment to nonsupernatural causes often extends to every other realm of life. Not all evolutionists are atheists, but evolution by purely natural causes is atheistic at its core. All explanations must be naturalistic. If there is a God, He must be arbitrarily kept out of science and scientific interpretations. Even if naturalistic explanations strain credulity, they are accepted and supernatural causes are categorically shunned.

What do we then make of those Christians who celebrate the dazzling design but choose to publicly ascribe it to an unknown "intelligent designer"? Far too complex to have resulted from purely natural causes, nature's intricacies are attributed to an intelligent cause, which could have been Buddha, a cosmic consciousness, space travelers, or the God of the Bible. The modern Intelligent Design Movement's leaders, some of whom are sincere Bible-believing Christians, have chosen as a strategy to expunge God the Creator from their dialogue in hopes of gaining a better hearing in the worlds of science and education. This "wedge" strategy has captured the fancy of some, but it has not been favored in court cases and administrative rulings. And it has not been blessed by the favor of the true Creator/God they have shunned.

The Creator deserves glory for His creative handiwork and majesty. He desires that we submit to His authority as Maker/Owner and not give His place to another. Rather than blessing individuals for their clever strategies, He punished His first steward over creation, banished His ungrateful chosen people, and abandons churches that veer from the truth. He does not, has not, and will not bless the misplaced efforts of His children who deny Him, no matter how sincere they might be.

Perhaps the wedge strategy will open the doors in school systems for more complete teaching in the future, but in the present we see the wedge working in a different manner. We see churches opening their doors to error—to secularism and false teaching—and closing them to serious Bible teaching as it relates to origins.

Dr. John Whitcomb has carefully elucidated this problem in the pages to follow. He is one of the great theologians of our day and a pioneer of creation scholarship. He sees clearly the dangers of bringing wrong thinking into the church. We would all do well to heed his insightful advice.

John Morris
President, Institute for Creation Research

Foreword

Ken Ham

Dr. John Whitcomb is one of Christianity's renowned modern-day apologists, especially in regard to defending a literal, six-day creation and a global Noah's Flood as recorded in Genesis. Over the decades Dr. Whitcomb has taught us something vital about the creation/evolution debate and biblical apologetics in general: although Romans 1 tells us that from looking at the creation it is obvious there is a God, Romans 10:17 points out that ultimately "faith comes from hearing, and hearing by the word of Christ." Coming to faith does not happen from evidence. As we often state in our ministry, there is no point in converting people to being just creationists, for creationists will end up in hell separated from their Creator forever if they do not receive the free gift of salvation from our Creator-Redeemer, the Lord Jesus Christ.

In recent times, what is termed the Intelligent Design Movement has gained some prominence for arguing against naturalism and proclaiming that there is an intelligence responsible for life. But its proponents will not name the intelligence! And although arguments for life being intelligently designed are overwhelmingly powerful, it is a fruitless exercise if we are not using these arguments in the context of presenting the Word of God so that people can learn how they can have a saving knowledge of their Creator and Redeemer.

It is my opinion that since the 1950s Dr. Whitcomb has been the world's leading theologically conservative Christian scholar who stands solidly on a literal Genesis. Even with his considerable academic background and intellect, however, people should be aware that his heart is not just to convince people that God is Creator and the Genesis account of history is literally true: he seeks to see people led to the foot of the Cross—to see them saved for eternity.

As Dr. Whitcomb shows in this book, making arguments for an intelligent designer poses a risk: it can open people up to seeking out a god who is a false god. After all, "The heart is deceitful above all things, and desperately wicked; who can know it?" (Jer. 17:9 NKJV). We are all inclined not to want the true God. Therefore, and as Dr. Whitcomb powerfully argues in his book, whenever we use intelligent design arguments, we should always do it in the context of introducing people to the true God and the authority of His Word. They need to understand that it is God's Word that convicts and saves. That is the important message found in Dr. Whitcomb's book on intelligent design.

Ken Ham
President, Answers in Genesis and
the Creation Museum

1

What Is Intelligent Design?

The Rise of the Intelligent Design Movement

At the end of the twentieth century, the academic world was hearing more and more about IDM—the Intelligent Design Movement. This growing movement held forth the proposition that the biological world could not have come into existence by mere undirected time and chance. Indeed, upon closer inspection, under the lenses of powerful microscopes, hitherto unimaginable, irreducible, specified complexity came to light within the cells of living things. Thus, Charles Darwin and his followers were in total error when they assumed that living cells were simple blobs of protoplasm that could easily "evolve" from lifeless chemicals floating in the earth's ancient oceans. As one writer expressed it, the incomprehensible, incomparable complexity of the cell was therefore a "black box" to Darwin![1]

The Intelligent Design Movement claims many outstanding scientists and philosophers. And, like detectives looking for clues or archaeologists searching for undeniably human artifacts, they have discovered new ways of detecting signs of intelligence.

Of course, there have been thousands of scientists—and thinking people in general—who have seen intelligent design in all the living world. In fact, only a tiny minority of people have ever been consistent atheists! For centuries, it has been recognized that blind, purposeless, meaningless chance could never have produced human minds. If our minds are merely products of chance and time,

---

[1] Michael J. Behe, *Darwin's Black Box* (New York: The Free Press, 1996).

11

an atheist would have no reason to expect people to believe that what he says is really true. Why not? Because "evolutionists must assume the preconditions of intelligibility in order to make any argument whatsoever; they must assume things like the laws of logic and uniformity of nature. But these preconditions of intelligibility do not comport with an evolutionary worldview; they only make sense if creation is true. Hence, we have an ultimate proof of creation: we know that biblical creation must be true because if it were not, we could not know anything at all."[2]

It therefore requires profound faith to be an evolutionist. No one has explained how the first speck of life could have evolved from lifeless chemicals, and nothing is evolving today. The famous second law of thermodynamics describes a universe that is everywhere and always proceeding downward to cosmic collapse, not upward to higher complexity.

There are trillions of fossils of plants, marine creatures, insects, reptiles, and mammals in the earth's crust, but no transitional forms connecting lower forms to higher forms have ever been found. Mutations are harmful, if not deadly. "Natural selection" can only select from living things that are here now; it cannot explain how the hundreds of thousands of living kinds got here in the first place. Complex body parts, such as legs and wings, require massive genetic information; but evolutionism has no concept of where such information came from.

Richard Dawkins, Simonyi Professor for the Public Understanding of Science at the University of Oxford, and perhaps the world's most prominent atheistic evolutionist, admits that "living objects ... look designed, they look overwhelmingly as if they were designed ... [and] Biology is the study of complicated things which give the impression of having been designed for a purpose." To this, John Lennox, professor of mathematics at the University of Oxford,

---

[2] Jason Lisle, *The Ultimate Proof of Creation* (Green Forest, AR: Master Books, 2009), 45-46.

replied, "Such statements provoke the question: Why? After all, if it looks like a duck, waddles like a duck and quacks like a duck, why not call it a duck? Why are such scientists not prepared to draw the obvious inference, and say that living things look as if they are designed precisely because they are designed?"[3]

Crucial Questions for ID

The Intelligent Design Movement has been widely popularized by Phillip E. Johnson (professor of law at the University of California, Berkeley) in his books, beginning with *Darwin on Trial* in 1991. Dr. Johnson, considered by many to be the chief architect of IDM, has clearly demonstrated that neo-Darwinian, materialistic evolutionism (which presupposes atheistic naturalism) simply cannot explain the nearly infinite complexity of living things. By inserting "the wedge" of intelligent design into the biological sciences, he is quite hopeful that materialistic naturalism will be uprooted in universities and public schools and that science and sociology textbooks will be purged of evolutionary distortions.

These are noble goals; and most of the argumentation of IDM books is, to this extent, on target. Every Christian should applaud legitimate efforts to restore sanity and reality to the study of ultimate origins in our public schools, our universities, and even in many of our "Christian" colleges.

The tragedy of the ID movement, however, is that it stops far short of honoring God's written revelation, the Bible. In fact, the book of Genesis as literal history seems to be an embarrassment to most of these scholars. Sadly, Johnson raised high the banner of religious neutrality for the entire ID movement when he wrote,

> For the present I recommend that we put the biblical issues to one side. The last thing we should want to do or seem to want to do is to threaten the freedom

---

[3] John C. Lennox, *God's Undertaker: Has Science Buried God?* (Oxford, England: Lion Hudson, 2007), 77.

13

of scientific inquiry. Bringing the Bible anywhere near this issue just raises the "Inherit the Wind" stereotype and closes minds instead of opening them. We can wait until we have a better scientific theory, one genuinely based on unbiased empirical evidence and not materialistic philosophy, before we need to worry about whether and to what extent that theory is consistent with the Bible.[4]

But how can we really help people understand the enormously crucial issue of our ultimate origin if we "put the biblical issues to one side"? Would listening to our God speak to us in His written revelation "threaten the freedom of scientific inquiry"? Would "bringing the Bible anywhere near this issue" actually "close minds instead of opening them"? And how long do we have to "wait until we have a better scientific theory … before we need to worry about whether and to what extent that theory is consistent with the Bible"?

Four years later, Johnson insisted:

Get the Bible and the Book of Genesis out of the debate because you do not want to raise the so-called Bible-science dichotomy. Phrase the argument in such a way that you can get it heard in the secular academy and in a way that tends to unify the religious dissenters. That means concentrating on, "Do you need a Creator to do the creating, or can nature do it on its own?" and refusing to get sidetracked onto other issues, which people are always trying to do. They'll ask, "What do you think of Noah's flood?" or something like that. Never bite on such questions be-

---

[4] Phillip E. Johnson, "How to Sink a Battleship," in *Mere Creation: Science, Faith and Intelligent Design*, ed. William A. Dembski (Downers Grove, IL: InterVarsity Press, 1998), 453.

cause they'll lead you into a trackless wasteland and you'll never get out of it.[5]

Is the "Bible-science dichotomy" something that God's people should be afraid of? Is it really God's plan for the true church to modify His creation message so that we "can get it heard in the secular academy"? Will such a drastic compromise really "unify the religious dissenters"? Are the magnitude and effects of the global flood of Genesis 6-9 part of a "trackless wasteland" into which we should refuse to be "sidetracked"?[6]

The Bible and ID

The Bible is completely clear on the issue of Intelligent Design: "For since the creation of the world His invisible attributes, His eternal power and divine nature, have been clearly seen, being understood through what has been made, so that they are without excuse." (Rom. 1:20). Here the apostle Paul informs us that Adam and Eve could discern God's "eternal power and Godhead" "by the things that are made," because "the invisible things of him" were "clearly seen"—not by animals but by men (beginning with our first parents)—"from the creation of the world."

But the fall brought about a profound change. When Adam and Eve rejected the clearly revealed will of God, they were overwhelmed by a sense of sin and shame they had never known; and they tried desperately to hide from their God: "Then the eyes of both of them were opened, and they knew that they were naked ... and the man and his wife hid themselves from the presence of the LORD God among the trees of the garden." (Gen. 3:7-8).

---

[5] "Berkeley's Radical: An Interview with Phillip E. Johnson" in *Touchstone* 15:5 (June, 2002), 41.

[6] Some, at least, would seem to answer these questions enthusiastically in the affirmative. Note the advice of John Wilson in "Unintelligent Debate," *Christianity Today*, September 2004, 62-68, who advises Intelligent Design advocates to tone down their rhetoric as it relates to theistic evolutionists and focus their attacks on young-earth creationists!

Every human from then until now (with the blessed exception of our Savior, Jesus Christ) has been conceived in sin (Ps. 51:5); and in those rare moments of spiritual conviction, we agree with the prophet Isaiah: "All of us like sheep have gone astray, each of us has turned to his own way" (Isa. 53:6). That is why it takes much more than brilliant ID arguments and the finite pressure of human rationalism to turn people back to God.

Optimism and Resistance

Some ID scholars, however, actually believe that within the next generation or so, they will succeed in accomplishing "a paradigm shift" in the entire academic/scientific world. For example, Phillip Johnson encourages his followers

> to inspire a lot of people to start doing intellectual work based on the right questions ... As the discussion proceeds, the intellectual world will become gradually accustomed to treating materialism and naturalism as subjects to be analyzed and debated ... Eventually the answer to our prime question will become too obvious to be in doubt.[7]

Then Johnson unveils his famous "wedge" strategy to change the thinking of materialistic scientists:

> The metaphor of a wedge portrays the modernist scientific and intellectual world, with its materialist assumptions, as a thick and seemingly impenetrable log. Such a log can be split wide open, however, if you can find a crack and pound the sharp edge of a wedge into it ... My own writings and speaking represents the sharp edge of this wedge. I make the

---

[7] Phillip E. Johnson, "The Intelligent Design Movement: Challenging the Modernist Monopoly on Science," in *Signs of Intelligence*, ed. William A. Dembski and James M. Kushiner (Grand Rapids: Baker Book House, 2001), 37-38.

first penetration, seeking always to legitimate a line of inquiry rather than to win a debate, measuring success by the number of significant thinkers I draw into the discussion, rather than by the conclusions that they draw for the present.[8]

Our success, Johnson assures us, "is all but inevitable ... [because] we are making a point of elementary logic that is irresistible once it is understood. The only obstacle to a breakthrough is the long standing prejudice [of materialism] ... A prejudice like that can be protected for a while, but in the end reason always breaks through."[9]

The same optimism characterizes the writings of most design theorists, because their official exclusion of the God of the Bible from their discussion really leaves them no other power system for changing the hearts and minds of materialists than their own finite intellects.[10] Jonathan Wells thinks that "biologists should trust their common sense." Surely, "they would be better off following the evidence wherever it leads ... Once [the neo-Darwinian monopoly in biology] is broken, we may expect to see dramatic scientific progress in understanding how embryos develop."[11]

Such thinking actually sets up an enormous barrier against the true Intelligent Designer of the universe, Jesus Christ the Lord. In effect, He is being told to stay out of the battle. Since ID experts believe they can handle the enemy with their own resources, He is not

---

[8] Ibid., 38. See appendix B for Henry Morris's objection to this "wedge" strategy.

[9] Johnson, "The Intelligent Design Movement," 40.

[10] See appendixes A and C for Henry Morris's concerns about ID's limiting the discussion to the mere existence of an intelligent designer and the unrealistic hopes that often motivate that limitation.

[11] Jonathan Wells, "Making Sense of Biology: The Evidence for Development by Design," in Signs of Intelligence, 127.

needed. But Christ told us: "Apart from Me you can do nothing [of eternal value and significance]" (John 15:5).

Mark Cadwallader, board chairman of Creation Moments Inc., concludes: "Even if you could store the contents of a thousand creation science books in your brain and had the ability to share that information in a clear, convincing way, it still wouldn't be enough to persuade even one person to abandon their belief in Darwinism or their unbelief in God."[12]

Is this really true? One of the most astounding and shocking discoveries of Intelligent Design theorists is not the almost infinite and irreducible complexity of living organisms but the almost total resistance to the implications of this on the part of materialistic scientists.

Two leading ID theorists, Benjamin Wiker and Jonathan Witt, stated their amazement in these terms:

> Why should we suffer any longer under the reign of
> materialism and its subspecies, Darwinism? There is
> no reason except an all-too-human intransigence in
> the face of mounting evidence ... Such blindness is
> actually a form of the most ancient of sins, pride; and
> this pride attacks science at its core. At the heart of
> the scientific enterprise is humility.[13]

These observations come close to God's perspective. Apart from the grace of God, the Bible tells us, men do not want to see the overwhelmingly obvious and universal signs of our Intelligent Designer. But this is nothing compared to the refusal of Jews and Gentiles (with rare exceptions) to see the deity and glory of the Son of God when He walked among men (John 1:14), speaking as no

---

[12] Mark Cadwallader, Creation Moments, August, 2008, www.creation-moments.com.

[13] Benjamin Wiker and Jonathan Witt, *A Meaningful World* (Downers Grove, IL: InterVarsity Press, 2006), 238, 246.

man ever spoke (John 7:46), performing signs never before seen on earth (John 3:2; 10:21), dying as no man has ever died (Mark 15:39; Rom. 3:21-26), and rising from the dead never to die again (Acts 1:1-3; 1 Cor. 15:1-19).

This is nothing less than a spiritual catastrophe: men refuse to see the light of the world! "This is the judgment, that the Light [God's only Son] has come into the world, and men loved the darkness rather than the Light, for their deeds were evil" (John 3:19). It is not a lack of ability to recognize, appreciate, honor, respect, and worship Him. It is a deliberate, intentional, profound, and continual refusal to see God in the face of Jesus Christ.

When our Lord healed a man born blind—a miracle that had never been experienced in human history (John 9:32-33)—He said: "'For judgment I came into this world, so that those who do not see may see, and that those who see may become blind.' Those of the Pharisees who were with Him heard these things and said to Him, 'We are not blind too, are we?' Jesus said to them, 'If you were blind, you would have no sin; but since you say, "We see," your sin remains'" (John 9:39-41).

But this is the ultimate issue: If people reject the Light of the world, in whose image and likeness we were originally created—which is *special revelation*—how can they possibly repent and believe by looking at the vastly dimmer light of *general revelation*?

In 2004, *World* magazine invited several leaders of the ID movement to "imagine writing in 2025, on the 100th anniversary of the famous Scopes 'monkey trial,' and explain how Darwinism has bit the dust, unable to rebut the evidence that what we see around us could not have arisen merely by time plus chance."[14]

In response, Phillip Johnson predicted that by 2025 naturalistic scientism will have "lost its hold on the popular and literary imag-

---

[14] "Darwin's Meltdown," *World* 19:13 (April 3, 2004), 34-47.

ination."[15] Darwinism will join Marxism and Freudianism "in the dustbin of history," and "the entire world [will seem] new and full of exciting possibilities."[16] By then, "sanity [will have] reasserted itself."[17]

Jonathan Wells suggested that by A.D. 2025, "Darwinian evolution [will be] little more than a historical footnote in biology text-books."[18] "Within a few short years [into the twenty-first century], Darwinism [will have] lost its scientific credibility and public funding ... By 2030, Darwinism [will be] effectively dead."[19]

William Dembski saw a wonderful kingdom coming to the world by the year 2025 because of the ID movement. "The primacy of in-formation throughout the sciences [will have] profound con-sequences for religion and faith ... With information as the primary stuff, there [will be] no limits on what the world can in principle reveal about God. Theists of all stripes [will therefore find] this newfound focus of science on information refreshing."[20]

Although the editors of *World* assured their readers that Johnson, Wells, and Dembski were just "having some fun," it seems obvious that they were writing in all sincerity: "Someday we will win!"

In response, David Roden observed: "Intelligent Design is a half-measure and wholly inadequate. Isn't the identity of the Intelligent Designer a necessary ingredient? Yet, your cover story offers no viewpoint from those who hold God's Word as the final au-thority."[21]

---

[15] Ibid., 36.

[16] Ibid., 37.

[17] Ibid., 38.

[18] Ibid.

[19] Ibid., 41.

[20] Ibid., 47.

[21] David Roden, letter to the editor, *World* 19:17 (May 1, 2004), 64.

The enormous complexity of living things was indeed "a black box" for Charles Darwin and his contemporaries. This has been carefully explained by Michael Behe in his book, *Darwin's Black Box.*[22]

But Professor Behe, a Roman Catholic theistic evolutionist,[23] like most Intelligent Design theorists, is amazingly naïve concerning the ultimate success of their campaign against materialistic evolutionism:

> I remain optimistic that the scientific community will eventually accept intelligent design, even if the acceptance is discreet and muted. The reason for optimism is the advance of science itself, which almost every day discovers new intricacies in nature, fresh reasons for recognizing the design inherent in life and the universe.[24]

While he is certainly correct about Darwin, the truth is that no one even today can fathom the significance of the complexities of the universe without God's help! In the central chapter of the book of Job, we read:

> But where can wisdom be found? And where is the place of understanding? Man does not know its value, nor is it found in the land of the living. ... it is hidden from the eyes of all living ... God understands its way, and He knows its place. ... And to man He said, "Behold, the fear of the Lord, that is wisdom; and to depart from evil is understanding." (Job 28:12-13, 21, 23, 28).

---

[22] Behe, *Darwin's Black Box* (New York: The Free Press, 1996).

[23] Cf. Ibid., 239.

[24] Michael J. Behe, "Darwin's Breakdown: Irreducible Complexity and Design at the Foundation of Life," in *Signs of Intelligence,* 101.

Apart from the revelation God has given to us of Himself in the Bible, everything in the universe remains a "black box." Not even the Intelligent Design Movement can penetrate this box, because they have officially denied the Lord Jesus Christ His rightful place in their thinking and thereby have rejected "all the wealth that comes from the full assurance of understanding, resulting in a true knowledge of God's mystery, that is, Christ Himself, in whom are hidden all the treasures of wisdom and knowledge" (Col. 2:2-3).

2

Who Is the Intelligent Designer?

Will Any "God" Do?

But who is the "god"—"the intelligent designer"—that ID theorists point to? Behe asserts:

> While I argue for design, the question of the identity of the designer is left open. Possible candidates for the role of designer include: the God of Christianity; an angel—fallen or not; Plato's demiurge; some mystical new age force; space aliens from Alpha Centauri; time travelers; or some utterly unknown intelligent being.[1]

When offered such choices to replace their materialistic reductionism, will many scientists today reject all of the false "intelligent designers" and turn to Christ as "the way, and the truth, and the life," and wholeheartedly agree with Him that "no one comes to the Father but through Me" (John 14:6)? No, this will not happen.

Instead, "in the last days difficult times will come. For men will be lovers of self, lovers of money, boastful, arrogant ... lovers of pleasure rather than lovers of God, holding to a form of godliness, although they have denied its power" (2 Tim. 3:1-2, 4-5).

---

[1] Michael Behe, "The Modern Intelligent Design Hypothesis," *Philosophia Christi*, Series 2, Vol. 3, No. 1 (2001), 165.

Can we take seriously, then, the prediction of Dr. Kenneth Poppe, executive director of the International Foundation for Science Education by Design, that

> in no more than ten years [from 2006], maybe as few as five, strict Darwinism will be a minority belief not only among people in society but also among science researchers and science educators. Within this time frame you will see a revolution where more and more politicians and board members vote to allow or encourage—in some cases even require—public school science teachers to cover some form of alternatives to natural evolution in their classes ... It is time for natural evolution to wave the white flag of surrender.[2]

This spirit of triumphalism, which pervades ID literature, is dangerous. It ignores God's written revelation concerning the true condition of the human heart/mind and the absolute necessity of the transforming work of the Holy Spirit of God through regeneration.

Furthermore, there can be no waving of "the white flag of surrender" on the part of materialistic evolutionism until the second coming of Christ. The Lord Jesus did not teach His disciples to pray for a widespread recognition of an unidentified Designer. Instead, He told His disciples to pray "in this way: 'Our Father who is in heaven, hallowed be Your name. Your kingdom come. Your will be done, on earth as it is in heaven'" (Matt. 6:9-10).

This is not defeatism. It is divine realism. What kind of kingdom will this be? Until the kingdom comes, how can we really help people who grope in the darkness of Darwinian evolutionism?

---

[2] Kenneth Poppe, *Reclaiming Science From Darwinism* (Eugene, OR: Harvest House Publishers, 2006), 289-90.

The True Designer

Intelligent Design theorists insist that they want Darwinian evolutionism to disappear and for truth to prevail in the academic and scientific world. They believe this can and must be done without any appeal to the Word of God. "In contrast to traditional creationism, the ID proposal relates only to a designer, without identifying the designer or specifying whether the designer is natural or supernatural."[3] Furthermore, "Intelligent design is not anti-evolution."[4] But note the infinite difference between the IDM strategy and God's plan: the ID strategy collapses in the presence of human depravity, while God's plan includes a perfect solution to this problem and will therefore succeed. That is why God can assure us that when His Kingdom comes "the earth will be full of the knowledge of the LORD as the waters cover the sea" (Isa. 11:9).

At last, everything in creation will be seen in the light of God's perspective, and all forms of evolutionary and materialistic thinking will be totally removed from the world. But only God can accomplish this, and it will be done exclusively through His Son, the Messiah of Israel, the King of Kings and the Lord of Lords. These are some of His qualifications: "The Spirit of the LORD will rest on Him, the spirit of wisdom and understanding, the spirit of counsel and strength, the spirit of knowledge and the fear of the LORD" (Isa. 11:2).

All other "gods" or "designers" have failed and will fail. As God announced to Jeremiah, "The gods that did not make the heavens and the earth will perish from the earth and from under the heavens" (Jer. 10:11).

---

[3] H. Wayne House, "Darwinism and the Law," in *Intelligent Design 101*, ed. H. Wayne House (Grand Rapids: Kregel Publishing, 2008), 212.

[4] Eddie N. Colanter, "Philosophical Implications of Neo-Darwinism and Intelligent Design: Theism, Personhood, and Bioethics," in *Intelligent Design 101*, 175.

To qualify as the true God, and worthy of worship, one must have created the entire universe! That narrows the competition to one Person—Jesus Christ, God's Son. As God continued to explain to Jeremiah, "It is He who made the earth by His power, Who established the world by His wisdom; And by His understanding He has stretched out the heavens" (Jer. 10:12).

But how do we know that this Creator is Christ, the Messiah of Israel? The New Testament is crystal clear on His identity.

> For by Him all things were created, both in the heavens and on earth, visible and invisible, whether thrones or dominions or rulers or authorities—all things have been created through Him and for Him. He is before all things, and in Him all things hold together. ... so that He Himself will come to have first place in everything. For it was the Father's good pleasure for all the fullness to dwell in Him (Col. 1:16-19).

The apostle John, speaking of "the Word" who "became flesh" (John 1:14) confirmed: "All things came into being through Him, and apart from Him nothing came into being that has come into being" (John 1:3; cf. Heb. 1:2).

But many Old Testament passages predicted that Christ our Creator would be "despised and forsaken of men, a man of sorrows and acquainted with grief" (Isa. 53:3; cf. Ps. 22:11-18; Zech. 12:10). This is exactly what happened when He came to earth and presented Himself as the Savior of the world. His claims and His gracious offer of the kingdom were rejected, and He was crucified. But God the Father honored His Son, and "highly exalted Him, and bestowed on Him the name which is above every name, so that at the name of Jesus EVERY KNEE WILL BOW, of those who are in heaven and on earth and under the earth, and that every tongue will confess that Jesus Christ is Lord, to the glory of God the Father" (Phil. 2:9-11).

Thus, ultimate truth cannot prevail in homes, schools, or governments until Christ returns. Until that day, God warns us: "See to it that no one takes you captive through philosophy and empty deception, according to the tradition of men, according to the elementary principles of the world, rather than according to Christ. For in Him all the fullness of Deity dwells in bodily form, and in Him you have been made complete, and He is the head over all rule and authority" (Col. 2:8-10).

For more than three years, the Son of God, the true Designer and Creator of all things in heaven and on the earth, personally (and through the preaching of John the Baptist, the twelve apostles and the seventy messengers) offered to Israel the magnificent kingdom that had been promised to them for many centuries (cf. Isa. 2; 11; 35; 65).[5]

This genuine offer was contingent on one thing only: repentance (i.e., a radical change of heart toward God) on the part of Israel. And no one had any valid reason for doubting His true identity. His claim to be Israel's divine Messiah was overwhelmingly confirmed by hundreds of spectacular sign-miracles. None of the "fingerprints of God" that we see today, from microscopic flagella to the galaxies above us, can compare to the persuasive power of those supernatural works. The Lord Jesus said, "The works which the Father has given Me to accomplish—the very works that I do—testify about Me, that the Father has sent Me" (John 5:36).

Nicodemus, the outstanding theologian of Israel, confessed to Jesus, "Rabbi, we know that You have come from God as a teacher; for no one can do these signs that You do unless God is with him" (John 3:2).

But the nation of Israel, with some exceptions, rejected these great messianic sign-miracles. Our Lord said of them: "If I had not done

---

[5] See Alva J. McClain, *The Greatness of the Kingdom* (Winona Lake, IN: BMH Books, 1959).

among them the works which no one else did, they would not have sin; but now they have both seen and hated Me and My Father as well" (John 15:24). The Jewish leaders even attributed His miracles to the power of Satan (John 8:48, 52).

What does all of this say to us concerning the Intelligent Design Movement? The conclusion is shocking indeed. The Bible tells us that even an acknowledgment of the divine origin of the sign-miracles of Jesus was not sufficient for spiritual salvation! To the brilliant Jewish rabbi Nicodemus, who rationalistically discerned the true source of Jesus' miracles and who risked his reputation by coming to Jesus one night to tell Him, "No one can do these signs that You do unless God is with him," our Lord replied: "Truly, truly, I say to you, unless one is born again he cannot see the kingdom of God" (John 3:2-3). He was so far from the kingdom he couldn't even see it! Why?

The answer is found in the three verses that immediately precede this amazing interview. (The chapter division tends to obscure the connection.) The apostle John wrote:

> Now when He was in Jerusalem at the Passover, during the feast, many believed in His name, observing His signs which He was doing. But Jesus, on His part, was not entrusting Himself to them, for He knew all men, and because He did not need anyone to testify concerning man, for He Himself knew what was in man. (John 2:23-25).

What did John mean by this? The answer comes in the next verses. "There was a man of the Pharisees, named Nicodemus" (3:1). Here was a clear example of a man who "believed in His name, observing His signs which He was doing" (John 2:23). Nicodemus not only believed in ID; he also believed in DM (divine miracles). But even this was vastly insufficient! Something of infinite and eternal significance was still missing, namely, childlike, genuine faith in Him, resulting in new birth (i.e., regeneration, salvation).

Throughout the Gospel of John, this theme keeps reappearing: to accept the divine origin of the miracles of Jesus was *essential* but totally *insufficient* for salvation. The Lord Jesus was not simply a great miracle worker. He was God's own Son, the Messiah and Redeemer of Israel, and the Savior of all mankind. What, then, was the purpose of His sign-miracles?

They were to attract attention to His words, His person, and His uniqueness as "the Lamb of God who takes away the sin of the world" (John 1:29). As He explained to unbelieving scribes who charged Him with blasphemy for pronouncing a paralytic man forgiven: "'But so that you may know that the Son of Man has authority on earth to forgive sins' — then He said to the paralytic, 'Get up, pick up your bed and go home'" (Matt. 9:6).

Although the majority of Israel's leaders attributed His miracles to Satan, there were five thousand men (plus their families) who wanted to acclaim Jesus as King when they beheld His healing miracles and ate the loaves and fishes He created for them (see John 6:1-15). But He was not deceived by this: "Truly, truly, I say to you, you seek Me, not because you saw [the true significance of the] signs, but because you ate of the loaves and were filled" (John 6:26).

Graciously and patiently He explained to them: "I am the bread of life; he who comes to Me will not hunger, and he who believes in Me will never thirst. But I said to you that you have seen Me, and yet do not believe" (John 6:35-36).

He continued to explain their desperate need of eternal life through faith in Him, but, "As a result of this many of His disciples withdrew and were not walking with Him anymore" (John 6:66).

Why ID Is Not Enough

At Jesus' triumphal entry into Jerusalem, multiple thousands of Jews "began to praise God joyfully with a loud voice for all the miracles which they had seen" (Luke 19:37b).

But again, as with the five thousand by the Sea of Galilee, out Lord was not deceived! When He saw the city, He "wept over it, saying, "If you had known in this day, even you, the things which make for peace! But now they have been hidden from your eyes" (Luke 19:41-42).

For these people, like Nicodemus, believing in ID—or even DM (divine miracles)—was not sufficient! Within hours, this same adoring crowd would be persuaded by their leaders to cry out to the Roman governor, "Crucify, crucify Him!" (Luke 23:21; cf. Matt. 27:20-26).

Do we really want God's best for people? Then we cannot settle for the acknowledgment of *any* god or the bringing in of *any* kingdom. With the illuminating and convicting work of the Holy Spirit, we must lead people to Christ alone, because He insisted: "I am the way, and the truth, and the life; no one comes to the Father but through Me" (John 14:6). If we accept His perfect redemption on the cross, confirmed by His bodily resurrection from the dead, He will take us all the way to the Father in heaven and to a full experience of the kingdom He has promised.

The reasons for massive, yes, global, human resistance to God's truth are clearly set forth in the Bible. The apostle Paul wrote, "For our struggle is not against flesh and blood, but against the rulers, against the powers, against the world forces of this darkness, against the spiritual forces of wickedness in the heavenly places" (Eph. 6:12). He is referring here, of course, to Satan and his vast demonic armies, to whom Adam surrendered his God-given dominion at the fall (see Gen. 1:26; 3:6).

In spite of the stupendous reality of Satan's judicial defeat by Christ at the cross (John 12:31; Col. 2:15; cf. Gen. 3:15), Satan is still (temporarily) "the ruler of this world" (John 12:31), and he "prowls around like a roaring lion, seeking someone to devour" (1 Pet. 5:8).

Until Christ returns to establish His kingdom, "the whole world lies in the power of the evil one" (1 John 5:19). Thus, "if our gospel is veiled, it is veiled to those who are perishing, in whose case the god of this world has blinded the minds of the unbelieving so that they might not see the light of the gospel of the glory of Christ, who is the image of God" (2 Cor. 4:3-4). If people do not want the true and living God in their lives, they have help from the unseen world of evil spirits to suppress this truth (cf. Judas Iscariot, John 13:21-30). The Intelligent Design Movement, of course, officially ignores this biblical perspective.

Another enormously important reality that plays no part in the basically secular IDM is believing prayer. The Lord Jesus Christ promised His disciples, "Whatever you ask in My name, that will I do" (John 14:13).

The qualification here, of course, is "in My name." This means that we must pray for things that are in harmony with His will (cf. John 15:7, 16; 16:23), just as the Lord Jesus Himself said to His Father when facing His wrath as man's substitute upon the cross: "yet not My will, but Yours be done" (Luke 22:42).

Praying for the spiritual conversion of people is in His will, because He is "not willing that any should perish, but that all should come to repentance" (2 Pet. 3:9 KJV).

Do we really think we can change the hearts and minds of people by the overwhelming logic and evidences for the intelligent design of the living world and the universe around us?

Evolutionist Richard Morris reluctantly admitted: "It is almost as though the universe had been consciously designed in such a way that life would be inevitable."[6] And the famous atheist at Oxford University in England, Richard Dawkins, stated, "Biology is the

---

[6] R. Morris, *The Fate of the Universe* (New York: Playboy Press, 1982), 28. Cited by Frank Sherwin, "An Evolutionist Becomes a Creationist Parasitologist," in *Persuaded by the Evidence*, ed. Doug Sharp and Jerry Bergman (Green Forest, AR: Master Books, 2008), 205.

study of complicated things that give the appearance of having been designed for a purpose."[7]

How can we really help such people? Christ our Lord and Savior told us, "Apart from Me you can do nothing" (John 15:5). During the sixty-eight years of my Christian life, I have discovered increasingly (but far from completely) how true this is. If God does honor our efforts to bring people to Him, we dare not congratulate ourselves, "for it is God who is at work in you, both to will and to work for His good pleasure" (Phil. 2:13).

But what really happens when an atheist is finally won over to the Intelligent Design view?

> In 2004 the academic world was rocked by the news that a prominent atheist had changed his mind. For the past half century, the name of philosopher Antony Flew was virtually synonymous with atheism. But now he has decided there is a God after all. What brought such an entrenched atheist to change his mind? The scientific case for Intelligent Design. Investigation of DNA "has shown, by the almost unbelievable complexity of the arrangements which are needed to produce (life), that intelligence must have been involved," Flew says in a video ("Has Science Discovered God?" The Institute for Metascientific Research, 2004). Though atheist colleagues were outraged by his change of mind, Flew replied calmly, "My whole life has been guided by the principle of Plato's Socrates: Follow the evidence, wherever it leads."[8]

---

[7] Richard Dawkins, *The Blind Watchmaker* (London: Norton, 1987), 1. Cited in *Persuaded by the Evidence*, 205-6.

[8] Nancy Pearcey, *Total Truth* (Wheaton, IL: Crossway Books, 2005), 498.

Tragically, however, "Mr. Flew still does not accept any revealed religion, including Christianity. He has simply become a 'theist,' or, as he says, a 'deist,' believing that God created the world, but no longer has a personal relationship with it."[9]

All of us should be pleased when any level of truth replaces any kind of error. But where does the redemptive work of our Lord Jesus Christ fit into such "conversions"? The last thing mankind needs is a revival of deism.

James J. S. Johnson explains that

> the problem, despite the positive contributions of IDMers ... is that what is sacrificed ... exceeded the benefits achieved, generally speaking. The payoff is like spending a dollar to gain a dime. A forensic logic technique is gained (apologetically speaking), yet the exorbitant price paid therefore is a functional withdrawal from the five doctrinal 'solas' of Biblical truth recovered by the Protestant Reformation (i.e., sola Scriptura, solo Christo, sola fide, sola gratia, and soli deo gloria). What net good is that, if we really care about transmitting truth to our neighbors?[10]

---

[9] Gene Edward Veith, "Flew the coop," *World* 19:50 (Dec. 25, 2004), 22. Flew is one example cited by Jerry Bergman of those who have been converted from atheism to theism due to ID. See Jerry Bergman, "Design Leads to Theism," *Creation Matters* 13:3 (May/June 2008), 1-3.

[10] James J. S. Johnson, "Shades of the Enlightenment," www.icr.org/I/pdf/research/NeoDeist_Intell_Design_Movt.pdf

3

Intelligent Design or the Gospel?

If we truly love people (that is, do for them what is best in the light of eternity, no matter what the price or cost may be to us), we must patiently, prayerfully and consistently tell them God's answers to the questions of ultimate origins, meaning, and destiny.

I will be forever grateful that the man God used to rescue me from materialistic evolutionism at Princeton University in 1943 did not apply a rationalistic "wedge" to my mind by the use of lengthy, complex—though perfectly valid—arguments for Intelligent Design. That man was Dr. Donald B. Fullerton, a 1913 graduate of the university and a veteran missionary to India and Afghanistan, who established the Princeton Evangelical Fellowship in 1931. This campus ministry continues to the present day.[1]

Indeed, to understand that the entire universe is the product of an Intelligent Designer is an *essential* foundation for the study of ultimate origins. But it is only the very bottom rung of the ladder of creation truth. It is vastly *insufficient!* It is an outwardly beautiful bridge that attracts people to escape from the barren wasteland of atheism and naturalism. But it is a bridge that is broken at the other end!

---

[1] My unpublished account of my conversion is entitled, "Priorities in Presenting the Faith—The Conversion of an Evolutionist." It is available through Whitcomb Ministries (www.whitcombministries.org).

To honor God and to bring full light into the vital question of where everything came from, one must honor His self-revelation in the Bible with its focus on the true identity and sacrificial work of the Savior of the world. One also must accept what He taught us concerning cosmic, geologic, and biologic origins in Genesis 1 and 2, the world-transforming curse of Genesis 3, and the global flood of Genesis 6 to 9.

Dr. Terry Mortenson explains:

> The ID movement is only focusing on design in creation and overlooking the obvious witness in creation to God's wrath outpoured at the Fall and the Flood. Additionally, they apparently fail to see ... that philosophical naturalism controls geology and astronomy as much as, if not more than, it controls biology, and that naturalism did not take control of science through Darwin but through old-earth geology and astronomy half a century earlier. Ultimately, the age of the earth controversy is not just a philosophical argument; rather, old-earth geology and old-universe astronomy, like evolutionary biology, are massive assaults on the authority and clarity of the Word of God.[2]

The Son of God—through whom God the Father "made the world" (Heb. 1:2); by whom "all things were created, both in the heavens and on earth" (Col. 1:16); the One who "is before all things" and by whom "all things hold together" (Col. 1:17); the One without whom "nothing came into being that has come into being" (John 1:3); the One who "was in the world, and the world was made through Him" (John 1:10); the "one Lord, Jesus Christ, by whom are all things, and we exist through Him" (1 Cor. 8:6); the One "in whom

---

[2] Terry Mortenson, "Boundaries on Creation and Noah's Flood" in *The Genesis Factor*, ed. Ron J. Bigalke, Jr. (Green Forest, AR: Master Books, 2008), 70.

are hidden all the treasures of wisdom and knowledge" (Col. 2:3)—the ultimate Intelligent Designer, has been practically ignored by those who write so eloquently of "the intelligent design" of all things.[3]

Paul's Appeal in Athens

Did the Apostle Paul ever appeal to Intelligent Design when he confronted unbelievers? Yes, but only in an introductory way. For example, at the Areopagus (i.e., Mars Hill) in Athens, he declared:

> For in Him we live and move and exist, as even some of your own poets have said, "For we also are His children." Being then the children of God, we ought not to think that the Divine Nature is like gold or silver or stone, an image formed by the art and thought of man. (Acts 17:28-29)

But for the members of Athens' city court to have agreed with Paul about the obvious fact of natural revelation would have accomplished nothing for their eternal salvation. And Paul knew this! He therefore concluded, "God is now declaring to men that all people everywhere should repent [i.e., to make a radical change of heart and mind about the holiness of God and the sinfulness of man]" (Acts 17:30; see also Christ's command that "that repentance for forgiveness of sins would be proclaimed in His name to all the nations" [Luke 24:47] and Paul's practice of declaring to all people "that they should repent and turn to God, performing deeds appropriate to repentance" [Acts 26:20]).

Why should these Athenian leaders "repent"? Answer: "Because He has fixed a day in which He will judge the world in righteousness through a Man whom He has appointed [i.e., the resurrected Jesus, whom Paul had presented for several days in the marketplace; Acts

---

[3] See appendixes E and F for helpful critiques of the ID Movement, as well as the enlightening exchange between Henry Morris and William Dembski in appendix D.

17:17-18], having furnished proof to all men by raising Him from the dead" (Acts 17:31).

What was their response to this shocking statement?

> Now when they heard of the resurrection of the dead, some began to sneer, but others said, "We shall hear you again concerning this." So Paul went out of their midst. But some men joined him and believed, among whom also were Dionysius the Areopagite and a woman named Damaris and others with them. (Acts 17:32-34).

Some believed! They were transformed forever by the grace of God through the convicting and illuminating work of the Holy Spirit. But how did this happen? The contemporary Intelligent Design Movement needs to ponder this statement. Without faith in the substitutionary death and bodily resurrection of the Son of God, there can be no genuine change of heart, no eternal salvation.

God's requirement for spiritual salvation is not belief in Intelligent Design. All of the religious leaders of Israel believed in ID. But they crucified the Designer! "You believe that God is one. You do well; the demons also believe, and shudder" (James 2:19).

What, then, does one have to believe to be eternally saved?

> If you confess with your mouth Jesus as Lord, and believe in your heart that God raised Him from the dead, you will be saved; for with the heart a person believes, resulting in righteousness, and with the mouth he confesses, resulting in salvation. (Rom. 10:9-10).

It is truly amazing that anyone in Athens would believe the gospel of Jesus Christ! "Now all the Athenians and the strangers visiting there used to spend their time in nothing other than telling or hearing something new" (Acts 17:21). When they heard that Paul "was preaching Jesus and the resurrection ... they took him and brought him to the Areopagus, saying, 'May we know what this new teaching is which you are proclaiming? For you are bringing some strange things to our ears; so we want to know what these things mean'" (Acts 17:18-20).

Like many Christians today, Paul might have replied, "I really do not want to shock and offend you by discussing these 'strange things' about 'Jesus' and 'resurrection.' Let's just agree on something more obvious and logical, namely, the abundant evidence for the existence of an Intelligent Designer of the world."

This would have constituted a powerful wedge into the gross idolatry that dominated the lives and fortunes of so many Athenians. Yet how awful would have been this compromise of the true and saving gospel of Jesus Christ our Lord!

But how could these Athenian politicians and philosophers have believed in Christ's redemptive work if they had never seen Him? The answer is clear. The Lord Jesus said to doubting Thomas, "Blessed are they who did not see, and yet believed" (John 20:29). He had previously explained to the disciples: "And He [the Holy Spirit], when He comes, will convict the world concerning sin and righteousness and judgment" (John 16:8). Only the third person of the triune Godhead can enable people to see the glory and the holiness of an invisible God. Of Moses it was written: "By faith he left Egypt ... for he endured, as seeing Him who is unseen" (Heb. 11:27). This is one of the Spirit's unique ministries to human beings.

These realities cannot be examined empirically in a test tube or through a telescope. They must be believed: "So then [saving] faith cometh by hearing, and hearing by the word of God" (Rom. 10:17 KJV). This is how Peter could write to "aliens, scattered throughout Pontus, Galatia, Cappadocia, Asia, and Bithynia" (1 Pet. 1:1), saying, "Though you have not seen Him, you love Him, and though you do not see Him now, but believe in Him, you greatly rejoice with joy inexpressible and full of glory, obtaining as the outcome of your faith, the salvation of your souls" (1 Pet. 1:8-9).

Salvation through Christ cannot be seen, but the intelligent design of the universe and world that surround us can be seen. Indeed, "since the creation of the world His invisible attributes, His eternal power and divine nature, have been clearly seen, being understood through what has been made, so that they are without excuse" (Rom. 1:20). Animals cannot see "the work of His hands" (Psalm 19:1); but human beings, bearing the image and likeness of God through creation (cf. Gen. 1:26), are fully capable of doing so and are responsible to their Creator for seeing and responding to Him through His glorious works.

Amazingly, our Lord informed us that physically blind people are fully capable of "seeing" God, but many of those who have 20/20 vision are blinded to His majesty and grace! When He healed a man born blind in Jerusalem, Jesus explained:

> "For judgment I came into this world, so that those who do not see may see, and that those who see may become blind." Those of the Pharisees who were with Him heard these things and said to Him, "We are not blind too, are we?" Jesus said to them, "If you were [physically] blind, you would have no sin; but since you say, 'We see,' your sin remains." (John 9:39-41).

Paul in Corinth

After his ministry in Athens, Paul journeyed west and south to Corinth, where he spent eighteen months (Acts 18:1-11). This notoriously immoral city also was obsessed with the "wisdom" of the Greeks, though the Athenians probably would have viewed them as being on a lower level than themselves in this respect.

What was Paul's strategy for reaching people for Christ in this city? Did he confront the Corinthians with spectacular and undeniable "design" arguments to win them to the Savior? No. Paul wrote,

> And when I came to you, brethren, I did not come with superiority of speech or of wisdom, proclaiming to you the testimony of God. For I determined to know nothing among you except Jesus Christ, and Him crucified. I was with you in weakness and in fear and in much trembling, and my message and my preaching were not in persuasive words of wisdom, but in demonstration of the Spirit and of power, so that your faith would not rest on the wisdom of men, but on the power of God. (1 Cor. 2:1-5)

Why did he do this? The apostle explained:

> There were not many wise according to the flesh, not many mighty, not many noble; but God has chosen the foolish things of the world to shame the wise, and God has chosen the weak things of the world to shame the things which are strong, and the base things of the world and the despised God has chosen, the things that are not, so that He may nullify the things that are, so that no man may boast before God. (1 Cor. 1:26-29)

Why is this so? It is because "The word of the cross is foolishness to those who are perishing ... For it is written, 'I will destroy the wisdom of the wise, and the cleverness of the clever I will set aside [Isa. 29:14]'" (1 Cor. 1:18-19).

Paul then asks,

> Where is the wise man? ... Has not God made foolish the wisdom of the world? For since in the wisdom of God the world through its wisdom did not come to know God, God was well-pleased through the fool-

ishness of the message preached to save those who believe. For indeed Jews ask for signs [cf. Matt. 12:38-42] and Greeks search for wisdom; but we preach Christ crucified, to Jews a stumbling block and to Gentiles foolishness, but to those who are the called, both Jews and Greeks, Christ the power of God and the wisdom of God. Because the foolishness of God is wiser than men. (1 Cor. 1:20-25)

In Lystra (Acts 14:15-17) and even in Athens (Acts 17:22-29) it was appropriate for Paul to introduce his gospel presentation with design arguments.

But Corinth—like the Western world today—was so deeply poisoned by philosophical pride and moral perversion that a direct confrontation with the work of the Savior was essential and urgent.

Essential but Insufficient

There are so many powerful design arguments available today, in the providence of God, that very impressive books can be written against atheism.[4] But my deep and abiding concern about the Intelligent Design Movement is that even when its most undeniable evidences are brilliantly presented, genuine spiritual revival does not follow. Hearts and lives are not being transformed. Eternal salvation comes to people exclusively through the Bible: "So then faith cometh by hearing, and hearing by the word of God" (Rom. 10:17 KJV). Intelligent design is *essential* to biblical Christianity, but it is not *sufficient*.

As Paul explained to the Christians in Rome:

---

[4] See, e.g., John Blanchard, *Does God Believe in Atheists?* (Auburn, MA: Evangelical Press, 2000); Norman Geisler and Frank Turek, *I Don't Have Enough Faith to Be an Atheist* (Wheaton, IL: Crossway Books, 2004); and Antony Flew, *There Is A God: How the World's Most Notorious Atheist Changed His Mind* (New York, NY: HarperCollins, 2008).

"THE WORD IS NEAR YOU, in your mouth and in your heart" [cf. Deut. 30:14]—that is, the word of faith which we are preaching, that if you confess with your mouth Jesus as Lord, and believe in your heart that God raised Him from the dead, you will be saved; for with the heart a person believes, resulting in righteousness, and with the mouth he confesses, resulting in salvation. ... for "WHOEVER WILL CALL ON THE NAME OF THE LORD WILL BE SAVED." (Rom. 10:8-10, 13)

May it be our goal in life as Christians to tell people everywhere that Jesus Christ the LORD is our Intelligent Designer and that by humble acceptance of His gracious gift of eternal life, based upon the price He paid upon the cross, confirmed by His bodily resurrection, we may know that our sins have been forgiven and that we will spend all eternity with Him.

"For God so loved the world, that He gave His only begotten Son, that whoever believes in Him shall not perish, but have eternal life" (John 3:16).

Appendix A

Neocreationism[1]

Henry M. Morris

Creationism is being fitted for new clothes today by a number of very articulate writers and speakers, and it is hoped by many that this will help it gain acceptance in the elite company of academics who have heretofore opposed it. One leader of the opposition to any form of creationism, Dr. Eugenie C. Scott, Executive Director of the National Center for Science Education, calls this development *neocreationism*.

> Phrases like "intelligent design theory," "abrupt appearance theory," "evidence against evolution," and the like, have sprung up, although the content of many of the arguments is familiar. This view can be called "neocreationism."[2]

Scott notes that the arguments for neocreationism are the same arguments that have been used by traditional creationists for many years. The new clothing is not so much what has been added, but what has been taken off.

> Neocreationists are by no means identical to their predecessors, however ... Neither biblical creationists

---

[1] Copyright © Institute for Creation Research. Used by permission. Morris, Henry M. 1998. Neocreationism. *Acts & Facts.* 27 (2). All Scripture quotations are from the KJV.

[2] Eugenie C. Scott, "Creationists and the Pope's Statement," *Quarterly Review of Biology* (Vol. 72, December 1997), 403.

nor theistic evolutionists ... Most of them are "progressive creationists."[3]

This new creationism is really not very new, except perhaps for the terminology. Progressive creationists, as well as traditional creationists, have been documenting intelligent design (that is, the magnificently organized complexity of every living creature) and "abrupt appearance" (that is, the complete absence of any true transitional forms in the fossil record) for well over 150 years.

But note what is missing. The neocreationists are not "Biblical creationists," Scott says. They may believe that the Bible is the Word of God, but they assume its testimony is irrelevant to their arguments. As Nancy Pearcey says:

> Design theory is also redefining the public school debate. At issue is not the details of evolution versus the details of Genesis; it's the stark, fundamental claim that life is the product of impersonal forces over against the claim that it is the creation of an intelligent agent.[4]

Now, this approach is not really new, either. During the past quarter century, ICR scientists have participated in well over 300 creation/evolution debates with university professors on college and university campuses, and each debate is intentionally framed to deal *only* with the scientific evidences, never with "the details of Genesis." Other creation lectures have been given on hundreds of campuses and scientific meetings with the same format, dealing only with science.

---

[3] Ibid.

[4] Nancy Pearcey, "Debunking Darwin," *World* (Vol. 11, March 1, 1997), 14.

In fact, ICR has also published a number of books[5] that present the case for creation strictly from a scientific perspective with no reference to religion. These debates and books have been successful in winning many individual scientists and others to belief in creation and frequently as a tool in winning them eventually to saving faith in Christ.

But what it will not do is displace evolutionism as the reigning paradigm in the intellectual community. One form or another of evolutionism, either atheistic or pantheistic, has been the reigning paradigm in every age since the beginning of human history (with one exception), and the prophetic Scriptures indicate that it will still be so when the Lord Jesus Christ returns at the end of this age to set up His own eternal kingdom.[6] That one exception consists of those small communities in many different nations and times who have believed in a personal Creator God who created all things, and who has revealed His purposes in creation and redemption through His written word, the Holy Scriptures.

In more modern times, William Paley popularized the design argument with his great book, *Natural Theology*, first published in 1802, profoundly influencing the English speaking world of his day—even including Charles Darwin! The book began with a detailed description of the "irreducible complexity" of a functioning watch, noting that even the most rabid skeptic would acknowledge that the watch—or at least its prototype—must have been designed and made by a skilled watchmaker. Just so, he argued persuasively, the much more complex universe required a universe-maker. These themes of intelligent design are compellingly developed at great length in Paley's 402-page book.

---

[5] The most recent of these is *Science and Creation*, Volume II in *The Modern Creation Trilogy*, by Henry M. Morris and John D. Morris (Green Forest, Arkansas: Master Books, 1996), 343 pp.

[6] For documented evidence of the age-long, worldwide dominance of evolutionism, see *The Long War Against God*, by Henry M. Morris (Grand Rapids: Baker Book House, 1989), 344 pp.

Darwin, however, wanted to find a way to escape Paley's conclusion, not for scientific reasons, but because he refused to accept a God who would condemn unbelievers like his father to hell.[7] Many modern Darwinians now follow him in maintaining that what appear to be evidences of design can also be explained by natural selection.

Richard Dawkins, Professor of Zoology at Oxford University, is the most articulate present-day advocate of neo-Darwinism, which maintains that evolution proceeds gradually through the preservation of small beneficial mutations by natural selection. Dawkins, a doctrinaire atheist, has published an influential book called, *The Blind Watchmaker*. Dawkins comes down hard on "fundamentalist creationists" but even harder on modern anti-Darwinists who try to insert God somehow into the "science" of origins.

> I suppose it is gratifying to have the Pope as an ally in the struggle against fundamentalist creationism. It is certainly amusing to see the rug pulled out from under the feet of Catholic creationists such as Michael Behe. Even so, given a choice between honest to goodness fundamentalism on the one hand, and the obscurantist, disingenuous doublethink of the Roman Catholic Church on the other, I know which I prefer.[8]

Dawkins is gloating over the fact that the Pope is an evolutionist,[9] but he is also impatient with the Pope's insistence that the human

---

[7] Charles Darwin, *Autobiography*. Edited by Nora Barlow (New York: Norton, 1969), 87.

[8] Richard Dawkins, "Obscurantism to the Rescue," *Quarterly Review of Biology* (Vol. 72, December 1997), 399.

[9] Ever since the publication of Pope John Paul II's October 1996 message on evolution, there has been controversy over what he actually said. The actual official English translation of his speech appeared in the October 30 edition of *L'Osservatore Romana*, and it does indeed affirm that he said that

soul has been "created." *Everything*, according to Dawkins and the modern neo-Darwinians, is attributable solely to the action of time and chance on matter, so that what *appears* to be evidence of design is really evidence of the creative power of random mutation and natural selection. Although Dawkins calls Behe a creationist, Behe himself claims to be an anti-Darwinian evolutionist.

More and more evolutionary biologists these days, in fact, are rejecting neo-Darwinism, acknowledging that the gaps in the fossil record (which have repeatedly been emphasized by creationists ever since Darwin's day, especially by the scientists representing the creation revival of the past four decades) make gradual evolution very hard to defend. Very few of these (if any) are becoming creationists, however—not even neo-creationists. The evidence of "abrupt appearance" is interpreted by them as "punctuations" in the "equilibrium" of the natural world. The increasing complexity of organisms in so-called evolutionary history is not interpreted as coming from intelligent design but as order emerging from chaos, probably by the mechanism of so-called "dissipative structures."[10]

Other evolutionists recognize that there is, indeed, evidence of intelligent design in the world, but they take it as evidence of Gaia (the Greek Earth goddess, or Mother Nature) or of some "cosmic consciousness." This New Age movement is essentially a return to ancient evolutionary pantheism, a complex of religions now growing with amazing rapidity all over the world. Thus Darwinians interpret the evidence of design in nature as natural selection, punctuationists interpret it as order through the chaos of dissipative structures, and New Age evolutionists interpret it as the intelligence of Mother Earth.

"the theory of evolution is more than a hypotheses" (Catholic News Service, November 19, 1996). He also spoke of "several theories of evolution," but by this he was referring mainly to the "materialist, reductionist, and spiritualist interpretations."

[10] See my article, "Can Order Come Out of Chaos?" "Back to Genesis" No. 102, ICR *Acts & Facts*, June 1997, 4 pp.

Getting people to believe in "intelligent design" is, therefore, neither new nor sufficient. People of almost every religion (except atheism) already believe in it. The only ones who do not, the atheists, have rejected it in full awareness of all the innumerable evidences of design in the world.

These cannot be won by intellectual argument, no matter how compelling. As Isaac Asimov said:

> Emotionally, I am an atheist. I don't have the evidence to prove that God doesn't exist, but I so strongly suspect he doesn't that I don't want to waste my time.[11]

King David, by divine inspiration, had a comment on the attitude of such atheists: "The fool hath said in his heart, There is no God" (Psalm 14:1, also Psalm 53:1). Similarly, in Romans 1:21, 22, the apostle Paul, discussing such people, said: "When they knew God, they glorified Him not as God, neither were thankful; but became vain in their imaginations, and their foolish heart was darkened. Professing themselves to be wise, they became fools."

This is strong language, and "design theorists" might recoil from using it, especially concerning their own academic colleagues, but it was God who said it! And intellectual fools are not won by intellectual arguments; if they are changed at all, it will be through some traumatic experience brought about by the Holy Spirit in answer to prayer.

Such Scriptures are speaking of those who are atheists "in their hearts." Like Asimov (and Dawkins, et al.), they are "emotional" atheists who have tried to ignore or subvert the real evidence with the pseudo-science of evolutionary speculation. There are, on the other hand, many "reluctant atheists" — those who have been so influenced by the doctrinaire atheists among their teachers and other

---

[11] Isaac Asimov, Interview by Paul Kurtz: "An Interview with Isaac Asimov on Science and the Bible," *Free Inquiry* (Vol. 2, Spring 1982), 9.

intellectuals, that they feel they *cannot* believe in the God of the Bible even though, in their hearts, they would like to believe.

People like this can be reached by sound evidence and reasoning. In our debates, for example, we know from many personal testimonies that a good number of students and young professionals in the audiences who had felt they had no choice but atheistic evolutionism, have indeed been won to solid creationism and soon to saving faith in Christ, at least in part by the scientific evidence. We hope this will be the experience of those who are now stressing "intelligent design," just as has often been true in the past.

But it will not be so if they stop with just the evidence for design and leave the Designer—the God of the Bible—out of it. Even though we intentionally limit our debates (and some of our books) to the *scientific* evidence, everyone in the audience and among our readers is well aware that we are really undergirding *Biblical* creationism (including recent Creation and the global Flood), because that is our clearly stated position.

But modern "intelligent design theorists" intentionally emphasize that, while they oppose materialism and Darwinian evolutionism, they are *not* arguing for Biblical creationism. At a conference on what was called "Mere Creation," held at Biola University in November 1996, the main speaker, Phillip E. Johnson, said in his concluding remarks:

> For the present, I recommend that we also put the Biblical issues to one side. The last thing we should want to do, or seem to want to do, is to threaten the freedom of scientific inquiry. Bringing the Bible anywhere near this issue ... closes minds instead of opening them.[12]

---

[12] Phillip E. Johnson, "Separating Materialist Philosophy from Science," *The Real Issue* (Vol. 15, November/December 1996). The "Mere Creation" conference involved over a hundred participants, practically all of whom were

In a widely reprinted article, a *New York Times* writer said:

> These new creationists avoid one pitfall of their predecessors by not positing, at least publicly, the identity of the creator. "My decision is simply to put it off," Mr. Johnson said, "and I recommend that to others."[13]

Now that may be all right as a temporary agreed-on constraint for a particular discussion—as in one of our scientific debates. But that cannot be the goal, and we need to be honest about this if we really believe the Bible to be the Word of God. The innumerable evidences of intelligent design in nature really do not point to theistic evolution or dissipative structures or Gaia, but if we stop our program without arriving at the true God of the Bible as the Creator of all things, then many converts to "design" will gravitate to one of these other beliefs and never come to know Jesus Christ as their Savior.

As faith without works is dead, so is design without the Designer!

---

either theistic evolutionists or progressive creationists. According to Eugenie Scott, "most of them have appointments at secular institutions" (op cit., p. 403).

[13] Laurie Goodstein, "New Light for Creationism," *New York Times*, December 21, 1997.

Appendix B

Design Is Not Enough![1]

Henry M. Morris

There is a strong movement among evangelicals today to emphasize "intelligent design" as the argument of choice against naturalism and Darwinian evolution. The movement is also called "mere creation" or "the wedge movement," the idea being to avoid controversial subjects such as the Biblical doctrine of creation in talking to evolutionists. Any discussion of a young earth, six-day creation, a world-wide flood and other Biblical records of early history will turn off scientists and other professionals, they say, so we should simply use the evidence of intelligent design as a "wedge" to pry them loose from their naturalistic premises. Then, later, we can follow up this opening by presenting the gospel, they hope.

But this approach, even if well-meaning and effectively articulated, will not work! It has often been tried in the past and has failed, and it will fail today. The reason it won't work is because it is not the Biblical method.

The famous book, *Natural Theology*, written two centuries ago by William Paley, profoundly impressed Charles Darwin with the evidence of design in nature. But it didn't lead him to Christ. Instead, he embarked on a lifelong quest to find an alternative to the Christian God as an explanation of apparent design. This quest led him to the "discovery" of *natural selection* as that desired alternative, and this concept soon became the worldview of the western world.

[1] Copyright © Institute for Creation Research. Used by permission. Morris, Henry M. 1999. Design Is Not Enough! *Acts & Facts.* 28 (7). All Scripture quotations are from the KJV.

There are, indeed, innumerable evidences of "intelligent design" in the world, from the stars in their courses to the insects in the forests. Isaac Asimov, certainly one of the century's outstanding scientists and writers, called the human brain "the most complex and orderly arrangement of matter in the universe."[2] But he still remained an atheist.

Sir Julian Huxley, probably the chief architect of neo-Darwinism, once made the following remarkable statement of faith in natural selection, after discussing the complexity of the horse:

> One with three million noughts after it is the measure of the unlikeliness of a horse—the odds against it happening at all. No one would bet on anything so improbable happening: and yet it has happened! It *has* happened, thanks to the working of natural selection ...[3]

An even more remarkable example of faith in the omniscient omnipotence of natural selection appears in the following recent statement:

> The genetic code is the product of early natural selection, not simply random, say scientists in Britain. Roughly 10^{20} genetic codes are possible, but the one nature actually uses was adopted as the standard more than 3.5 billion years ago ... it is extremely unlikely that such an efficient code arose by chance—natural selection must have played a role.[4]

---

[2] Isaac Asimov, "In the Game of Energy and Thermodynamics You Can't Even Break Even," *Smithsonian* (June 1970), 10.

[3] Julian Huxley, *Evolution in Action* (New York: Harper and Row, 1953), 46.

[4] Jonathan Knight, "Top Translator," *New Scientist* (Vol. 158, April 18, 1998), 15.

Thus natural selection not only "creates" new species, as Darwin thought, but even the very code by which life itself evolved and carries on. Although 100 billion billion different codes were possible choices, natural selection made the one right choice, and it did so before any life existed at all, so the reasoning goes. All hail the power of natural selection!

It is obvious that neither "intelligent design" nor "irreducible complexity" nor any other such euphemism for creation will suffice to separate a thoroughgoing Darwinian naturalist from his atheistic religion, in favor of God and special creation.

On the other hand, a goodly number of atheists may convert to pantheism through such arguments. The various ethnic religions (Hinduism, etc.) all accommodate design, and so do the modern "New Age" cults and movements. They agree that there must be some kind of cosmic consciousness in nature—call it Mother Nature, perhaps, or Gaia (the Greek goddess of the earth)—that enables the earth and the cosmos to organize themselves into complex systems.

> The very fact that the universe is creative, and that the laws have permitted complex structures to emerge and develop to the point of consciousness— in other words, that the universe has organized its own self-awareness—is for me powerful evidence that there is something going on behind it all. The impression of design is overwhelming.[5]

Design yes—but God, no! Davies is a very eminent astronomer and has received one of the famous Templeton prizes for relating science and religion, but he thinks modern evolutionary cosmology has

---

[5] Paul C. Davies, *The Cosmic Blueprint* (New York: Simon and Schuster, 1988), 203.

proved the universe has "no need for an external creator in the traditional sense."[6]

It should not surprise us that design is not enough, for this is what the Word of God tells us. Probably the two greatest passages on the evidences of intelligent design in nature are Psalm 19:1-6 and Romans 1:19-23—one in the Old Testament, one in the New. Let us, therefore, look briefly at these two passages, First, Psalm 19.

> The heavens declare the glory of God; and the firmament sheweth His handiwork. Day unto day uttereth speech, and night unto night sheweth knowledge. (vv. 1, 2)

Thus the created cosmos continually displays wonderful evidences of the glory and handiwork of God, for everyone in every nation to see and hear, night and day. Yes, but this very testimony becomes an indictment against them when they go on without believing Him.

The heavens do "declare the glory of God," but "all have sinned and come short of the glory of God" (Romans 3:23). The evidence of design may *impress* the soul, but it will not *save* the soul! But there is something that will, for it does not fall short at all.

> The law of the LORD is perfect, converting the soul: the testimony of the LORD is sure, making wise the simple. The statutes of the LORD are right, rejoicing the heart: the commandment of the LORD is pure, enlightening the eyes. The fear of the LORD is clean, enduring for ever: the judgments of the LORD are true and righteous altogether. (Psalm 19:7-9)

We must go to the Scriptures for salvation. The scientific evidence for design and creation and the Creator are vital to present to those

---

[6] Paul C. Davies, "What Hath COBE Wrought?" *Sky and Telescope* (January 1993), 4.

who do not know or believe the Bible (note Acts 14:15-17 and 17:22-29), but then they must go to the Scriptures if they would learn about the true God and His work of creation and redemption.

Note also the message built around Romans 1:19-23, also stressing the reality, but the inadequacy, of so-called natural revelation.

> For the invisible things of Him from the creation of the world are clearly seen, being understood by the things that are made, even His eternal power and Godhead; so that they are without excuse. (v.20)

In many marvelous ways, the fact of God and the nature of God are clearly revealed in His beautiful "poem" of creation (Greek, *poiema*, "things that are made"). Nevertheless, those who see it, "Professing themselves to be wise, (become) fools" (v. 22). In the ancient world, they "changed the truth of God [that is, His word, which is truth— John 17:17] into a lie, and worshipped and served the creature [or 'creation'] more than the Creator" (v. 25). These were the pantheistic evolutionists of old Babylon and Egypt and Greece and Rome.

And the modern New Agers are doing exactly the same thing. They see the wonderful evidences of design all around them, but instead of turning to the true Creator, the Lord Jesus Christ, they worship nature instead, attributing all these marvelous evidences of God's eternal power and Godhead to the creative cosmos. In so doing, they are utterly "without excuse," for the evidence of God is all around them.

They are without excuse, but they are also *without salvation!* The evidence of intelligent design does not bring them to Christ, but to Mother Nature. Scientific creationism, which incorporates the evidence of design along with the overwhelming evidence against any evolutionary substitute (whether Darwinian atheism or New Age Pantheism) is vitally important, but it must be either followed by or accompanied by a sound presentation of true Biblical creationism if it is to be meaningful and lasting.

We call this body of evidence and doctrine the study of scientific Biblical creationism. But this is still only the foundation, not the complete saving gospel. Jesus Christ must then be presented as not only the eternal Creator, but also as our redeeming Savior, living Lord, and soon-coming King. And that *is enough* for eternal salvation to all who believe and follow Him.

Appendix C

Insufficient Design[1]

Henry M. Morris

The modern Intelligent Design movement (ID) has been making substantial progress in recent years, at least in terms of public interest. As an evolutionist recently warned his colleagues:

> The success of the ID movement to date is terrifying. In at least 40 states, ID is being considered as an addition to the required science curriculum in public schools.[2]

The "terrified" author of this observation is Professor of Anthropology at Pennsylvania State University. He says he is being *stalked* by ID advocates!

> Now I know that I and my colleagues are being stalked with careful and deadly deliberation. I fear my days are numbered unless I act soon and effectively. If you are reading this, the chances are that you are in the same position.[3]

The editor of the prestigious magazine *Science*, in his lead editorial in a recent issue, expressed his alarm thus:

---

[1] Copyright © Institute for Creation Research. Used by permission. Morris, Henry M. 2006. Insufficient Design. *Acts & Facts.* 35 (3). All Scripture quotations are from the KJV.

[2] Pat Shipman, "Being Stalked by Intelligent Design," *American Scientist* (Vol. 93, November/December 2005), 502.

[3] Ibid., 501.

> Alternatives to the teaching of biological evolution are now being debated in no fewer than 40 states. Worse, evolution is not the only science under such challenge. In several school districts, geology materials are being rewritten because their dates for Earth's age are inconsistent with scripture (too old).[4]

The editor even entitled his diatribe "Twilight for the Enlightenment?"

Similar alarmist articles have been published in numerous other science journals and also in many popular magazines (such as *Newsweek*) and local papers. Our own *San Diego Union Tribune* in a lengthy lead editorial for November 21, 2005, called Intelligent Design "Voodoo Science" in the editorial title. The language seems inflammatory just about everywhere.

One writer becomes unreasonably virulent in his latest editorial.

> The 'Intelligent Design' movement is the most pernicious pseudoscience of our time. It seeks to undermine the teaching of evolution, at a minimum, but at its root is a broad attack on the nature of science itself ...[5]

He then calls ID "an ancient and long-discredited faith-based idea with zero scientific evidence."[6]

Is ID Really Intelligent?

The reason for calling attention to this almost universally negative reaction to the ID movement among leaders in science, education,

---

[4] Donald Kennedy, "Twilight for the Enlightenment?" *Science* (Vol. 308, April 8, 2005), 165.

[5] Kendrick Frazier, "Evolution and the ID Wars," *Skeptical Inquirer* (Vol. 29, November/December 2005), 4. Frazier is Editor of this magazine.

[6] Ibid.

law, journalism, and other fields is to note the unrealistic hope that ID leaders have about their movement. Christians have been pointing out for a very long time that the ubiquitous evidences for design in nature constitute strong evidences for God and creation. But atheists and other unbelievers have long hailed Darwinism as their deliverance from this constraint.

Now the ID people think that by distancing their movement from creationism and the Biblical God as the obvious Designer, they can make ID acceptable. They are learning, however, that opposition to ID is even stronger among scientists, if anything, than the opposition to straightforward creationism.

Many evolutionists now regard ID as a hypocritical form of creationism and thus really a religion rather than science.

Another skeptic has pointed out what he thinks is a very different reason for rejecting the main ID contention.

> According to Behe and Dembski, the more complex a system, the more likely it was designed — this is the essence of Point A in Behe's concept.
>
> Point B (irreducibility) in Behe's concept asserts that an IC system loses its function if even a single part is missing.[7]

That is, a system is irreducibly complex (IC) if it could no longer function if even one part is missing. That, according to these two leaders of the ID movement (Michael Behe and William Dembski) means it must have been intelligently designed.

But this particular writer opines that this would be proof that it was *not* designed by any kind of intelligence! Thus, it must have been assembled somehow by impersonal time and chance.

---

[7] Mark Perakh, "Does Irreducible Complexity Imply Intelligent Design?" *Skeptical Inquirer* (Vol. 29, November/December, 2005), 34.

> The simple fact is, though, that if an IC system has been designed, it is a case of *bad design*. If the loss of a single part destroys the system's function, such a system is unreliable, and therefore, if it is designed, the designer is inept.[8]

This is a clear example of specious reasoning, but Perakh belabors it at some length. It does lead, however, to an important conclusion. That is, mere complexity is not proof of design.

For example, a perfectly cubical object found in a pile of rocks, say, would certainly have been designed for some kind of purpose—say, as a toy block for a child to play with or as one of a pair of dice for a gambler to throw. An irregular rock in that same pile, on the other hand, would be much more complex and therefore more difficult to specify than the cube but it clearly would have been formed randomly by a hodgepodge of forces over a long period of time.

In other words, complexity in itself is not evidence of design. But if it is organized and purposive complexity, then it would surely seem to have been designed. Therefore, instead of wasting time and talent on evolutionary speculation as to how natural selection might have generated a particular animal, say, creationists believe that the scientist would more profitably have tried to determine *why* the Designer created such an animal.

In any case, evolutionists almost universally conclude that: "As currently promoted, ID theory is neither new nor good science."[9]

Creation and/or Design

The most serious deficiency in the ID movement, however, is its neglect of the most important of the alleged evidences for evolution—

---

[8] Ibid., 35.

[9] Michael F. Antolin and Joan M. Herbers, "Evolution's Struggle for Existence in America's Public Schools," *Evolution* (Vol. 55, December 2001), 2383.

that is, the problem of the fossils. These are the remains of billions and billions of once-living plants and animals now preserved in the sedimentary crust of the earth. These all give abundant evidence of suffering and death during all the supposed geological ages which they are supposed to depict.

Did the Designer do *that*? If so, just how and why? The only adequate answer is in the Bible, in its record of man's sin, the resulting global Curse and eventual Deluge. But the very purpose of the ID movement is to argue for intelligent design without reference to the Bible and the God of the Bible.

Without those factors, however, it would seem that the only alternative would be to assume the Designer to be a sadistic producer of global evil as well as the intelligent producer of irreducible complexity.

We so-called "Young-Earth Creationists" also have always believed and taught what seem to us to be irrefutable evidences of intelligent design in nature, but that is not enough. We simply have to take the Biblical record as God's Word, in which He has taught the real and total truth about origins, as well as about sin and death, then providing also the wonderful solution to all such problems in the glorious Gospel of our Lord and Savior Jesus Christ.

Whether these facts are considered scientific or not, they are *historical facts* which should be considered if *Truth* is the ultimate goal.

We appreciate the tremendous contribution the ID leaders have made to the origins question, but we feel we must urge them to believe the whole counsel of God and return to the true Biblical record of recent Special Creation, the Fall and Curse, the worldwide Flood, and the promised return of God in Christ to consummate His purposes in Creation.

Although it is unlikely that full-fledged creation will ever be accepted in public schools, it can be argued that Intelligent Design will not be accepted there either. Even if an occasional school board decides to insist on it, it would be a travesty to make teachers who don't believe it try to teach it.

But remember that government schools are unscriptural in the first place. The home is, Biblically speaking, ultimately responsible for the teaching of its youth. The original schools and colleges of our country were always either home schools or sponsored by Christians, with government schools "evolving" later.

If the options of homeschooling or religious schooling are not available (as was true for my own six children), then the parents should monitor what their offspring are being taught in the public schools and colleges and help them get it all back in Biblical perspective.

Two key Bible texts are appropriate in this connection. "Study to shew thyself approved unto God, ... rightly dividing the word of truth" (II Timothy 2:15). Then, "But sanctify the Lord God in your hearts: and be ready always to give an answer to every man that asketh you a reason of the hope that is in you with meekness and fear" (I Peter 3:15).

Appendix D

Morris and Dembski on Design

The February 2005 issue of the Institute for Creation Research's Acts and Facts *published Henry Morris's review of William Dembski's book,* The Design Revolution. *The review elicited a public response from Dembski entitled "Intelligent Design's Contribution to the Debate over Evolution: A Reply to Henry Morris," and was followed by Morris's private e-mail to Dembski. These documents are reprinted here with the permission of the parties involved.*

*****

The Design Revelation[1]

Henry Morris, Ph.D.

The Design Revolution is the title of a significant new book by William Dembski,[2] elaborating on the Intelligent Design (ID) movement which is being welcomed by many evangelicals today as the best response to Darwinism. The book is certainly impressive, with a daunting array of new terms. On the book jacket Phillip Johnson (the commonly accepted leader of the movement) said, "Bill Dembski poses all the tough questions that critics ask about intelligent design in biology, and brilliantly answers them all!"

---

[1] Copyright © Institute for Creation Research. Used by permission. Morris, Henry M. 2005. The Design Revelation. *Back to Genesis.* 194. All Scripture quotations are from the KJV.

[2] William Dembski, *The Design Revolution* (Downer's Grove, IL: Inter-Varsity Press, 2004), 334 pp.

However, it was disappointing that no subject index was included. Also, although Dembski quotes from numerous other writers, he gives no documentation for any of these often very relevant quotes.

Although he covers much ground already well explored by "young-earth creationists," he does not acknowledge this. On the other hand, he emphasizes that "intelligent design" is *not* "scientific creationism" in his chapter 3 (pp. 41-44). The chapter begins with the assertion: "Intelligent design needs to be distinguished from *creation science,* or *scientific creationism.*" Then, in the last paragraph of this chapter, he stresses that:

> ... the designer underlying intelligent design need not even be a deity. ... Unlike scientific creationism, intelligent design does not prejudge such questions as Who is the designer? or How does the designer go about designing and building things? (p. 44).

We disagree with this approach! We do appreciate the abilities and motives of Bill Dembski, Phil Johnson, and the other key writers in the Intelligent Design Movement. They think that if they can just get a "wedge" into the naturalistic mindset of the Darwinists, then later the Biblical God can be suggested as the "designer" implicit in the concept.

We occasionally have used a similar approach ourselves. For example, our creation/evolution debates on university campuses are set up to be strictly scientific debates, with no reference to Bible or religion. Normally the creationist side will "win," strictly on the basis of *scientific* arguments. However, the audiences all know that we on the creation side are actually Bible-believing Christians, so they interpret our scientific arguments in that context. Furthermore, we know that the Christians in the audience (usually in the sponsoring organization) will be active in follow-up ministry. We also have a few books, technical monographs, etc., that deal solely with the scientific aspects of the subject. Creationism can, indeed, be adequately justified just by scientific evidence and reasoning.

But what about the ID strategy? Even if one becomes a believer in intelligent design he is still unsaved until he receives—by faith—God in Christ as His personal Designer, Creator, and Redeemer. In fact, there are multitudes of creationists (in Islam and Judaism, for example, as well as in various cults) who still reject the Lord Jesus as God and Savior. Creation is the *foundation* of the saving Gospel of Christ, but not the whole structure. We have been commissioned to *"preach the gospel to every creature"* (Mark 16:15), not just the need for a designer.

Two Fallacies

Our concern with the intelligent design approach probably devolves upon two main factors. First, it is ineffective, no more convincing to evolutionists than is young-earth creationism; second, it is not really a new approach, using basically the same evidence and arguments used for years by scientific creationists but made to appear more sophisticated with complex nomenclature and argumentation. Not only are atheistic evolutionists (such as Dr. Eugenie Scott and the leading evolutionists who are board members of her National Center for Science Education) unimpressed by it, but so are many "Christian evolutionists" such as Dr. Ken Miller (the Catholic biologist at Brown University) and Dr. Howard Van Till (the Calvinist physicist at Calvin College). These latter scientists and their many colleagues are quite satisfied with believing that God instituted the evolutionary "process" and has allowed it to work on its own with no further "design" on His part.

The intelligent design movement has been quite successful in one aspect, however. Many Christians now seem to think that it has freed them from having to confront the Genesis record of a young earth and global flood. All they need to do, they have decided, is to believe in intelligent design. This result was surely not what Dembski and others intended, but that is what's happening.

Our other hesitation to get on this bandwagon is their use of the same arguments and evidences we Biblical creationists have used for years, while simultaneously trying to distance themselves from us. Our adherence to Biblical literalism is ridiculed by evolutionists, and the ID advocates would be embarrassed to be tarred with the same brush. In fact, Dembski goes so far as to say belief in evolution itself is okay, as long as it's not naturalistic. He opens his chapter 23 with the following:

> Intelligent design does not require organisms to emerge suddenly or to be specially created from scratch by the intervention of a designing intelligence. ... What separates intelligent design from naturalistic evolution is not whether organisms evolved or the extent to which they evolved but what was responsible for their evolution.[3]

It is not even necessary that the designing intelligence be God.

> Intelligent design is a strictly scientific theory devoid of religious commitments. Whereas the creator underlying scientific creationism conforms to a strict, literalist interpretation of the Bible, the designer underlying intelligent design need not even be a deity.[4]

Dembski himself may not believe such nonsense, but he is trying to build a very large tent, allowing anyone except pure materialists to take refuge there.

These well-meaning folks did not really invent the idea of intelligent design, of course. Dembski often refers, for example, to the bacterial flagellum as a strong evidence for design (and indeed it is); but one of our ICR scientists (the late Dr. Dick Bliss) was using this example in his talks on creation a generation ago. And what about our monographs on the monarch butterfly, the bombardier beetle, and many other testimonies to divine design? Creationists have

---

[3] Ibid., 178.

[4] Ibid., 44.

been documenting design for many years, going back to Paley's watchmaker and beyond.

Dembski uses the term "specified complexity" as the main criterion for recognizing design. This has essentially the same meaning as "organized complexity," which is more meaningful and which I have often used myself. He refers to the Borel number (1 in 10^{50}) as what he calls a "universal probability bound," below which chance is precluded. He himself calculates the total conceivable number of specified events throughout cosmic history to be 10^{150} with one chance out of that number as being the limit of chance. In a book[5] written a quarter of a century ago, I had estimated this number to be 10^{110}, and had also referred to the Borel number for comparison. His treatment did add the term "universal probability bound" to the rhetoric.

God's Revelation of Design

It thus seems premature to think of the intelligent design movement as a "revolution," for it is neither new nor convincing to the Darwinists it seeks to influence. There is indeed much evidence of design in nature and God's Word frequently refers to it. *"For the invisible things of Him from the creation of the world are clearly seen, being understood by the things that are made ... so that they are without excuse"* (Romans 1:20).

That is, those who refuse to see the evidence of God's handiwork in the things He made are inexcusable. One does not have to be an engineer or a probability mathematician to see that the animals and plants of the world—not to mention the stars in the heavens and the very laws of nature themselves—could never have evolved out of primeval nothingness. Evolutionists think that, if they can even *imagine* how things might have organized themselves into higher

---

[5] Henry M. Morris, *King of Creation* (San Diego, CA: CLP Publishers, 1980), 130-131; out of print. See *The Modern Creation Trilogy* (vol. 2 Green Forest, AR: Master Books, 1996), 168-175.

levels of complexity, that is sufficient proof that it must have happened!

Furthermore, the origins issue is mainly a historical question, not merely one related to the complexity of organisms. Not *"could* it happen?" but *"did* it happen?" The historical evidence for Creation and the Flood—and against evolution—especially as recorded in the Word of God, is so strong that the apostle Peter calls it *willful ignorance* not to accept it! (II Peter 3:3-6).

As far as the organized complexity of any living thing is concerned, the ancient challenge of Job is still relevant. *"But ask now the beasts, and they shall teach thee; and the fowls of the air, and they shall tell thee: Or speak to the earth, and it shall teach thee: and the fishes of the sea shall declare unto thee. Who knoweth not in all these that the hand of the Lord hath wrought this?"* (Job 12:7-9).

A school child can easily tell a rounded stone from a crafted arrowhead—one shaped by natural forces, the other by skilled human hands. Just so, the incredible organized complexity of even the simplest one-celled organism speaks clearly of intelligent design, and one should not need sophisticated rhetoric or math to recognize this.

We had best try to teach all who will listen with open minds the complete gospel of creation and redemption, not just argue the fine points of complexity. God has *"left not Himself without witness"* (Acts 14:17), and anyone of willing heart will hear.

Intelligent Design's Contribution to the Debate Over Evolution: A Reply to Henry Morris[1]

William A. Dembski

1 February 2005

In the spring of 1992, I had lunch with Michael Ruse during a symposium at Southern Methodist University. The symposium addressed Phillip Johnson's then recently published book, *Darwin on Trial*. Johnson and Ruse were the keynote speakers, with Johnson defending his critique of evolution, Ruse challenging it. My role, and that of several other speakers, including Michael Behe, Stephen Meyer, Fred Grinnell, and Arthur Shapiro, was to contribute to the primary discussion between Johnson and Ruse. (The symposium proceedings, under the title *Darwinism: Science or Philosophy?* are available through the Foundation for Thought and Ethics at www. fteonline.com.)

During our lunch conversation, Ruse commented that for all his disagreements with the young earth creationists, and Henry Morris in particular, he did give them credit for, as he put it, "keeping this issue alive." The "issue" here was the debate over biological evolution and, in particular, the possibility of design providing a viable alternative to existing materialistic accounts of evolution.

My own experience has abundantly confirmed Ruse's remark. In traveling outside the United States, I've found that evolutionary theory goes largely unchallenged. In the United States, by contrast, there remains widespread skepticism toward evolution. And even though intelligent design has emerged as the most visible banner under which evolution is now being challenged, the challenge would not exist without the efforts of Henry Morris and young earth creationists.

---

[1] This open letter is reprinted here by permission of Dr. William Dembski.

I myself would not be a design theorist today without them. To be sure, I am not a young earth creationist nor do I support their efforts to harmonize science with a particular interpretation of Genesis. Nonetheless, it was their literature that first got me thinking about how improbable it is to generate biological complexity and how this problem might be approached scientifically. A. E. Wilder-Smith was particularly important to me in this regard. Making rigorous his intuitive ideas about information has been the impetus for much of my research.

In his book *Darwin and Design* (Harvard University Press, 2003), Michael Ruse makes clear that the key question in the debate over biological evolution is not whether evolution is progressive but rather how biological complexity originated. Creationists have always, and rightly, kept this question at the forefront.

For these reasons, I regard Henry Morris as a great man. I've met most of the leading lights associated with his Institute for Creation Research (e.g., Duane Gish, John Morris, and John Baumgardner). Moreover, I corresponded in the 1980s with the late A. E. Wilder-Smith. Unlike many Darwinists and theistic evolutionists, young earth creationists have been extraordinarily gracious to me, and I've always tried to return the favor. I therefore regret never meeting Henry Morris in person. I hope still to do so in this life.

Despite my disagreements with Morris and young earth creationism, I regard those disagreements as far less serious than my disagreements with the Darwinian materialists. If you will, young earth creationism is at worst off by a few orders of magnitude in misestimating the age of the earth. On the other hand, Darwinism, in ascribing powers of intelligence to blind material forces, is off by infinite orders of magnitude.

Still, it will not do to paper over our differences. Intelligent design and creationism diverge at some key points. Morris recently described how he sees the disagreement. This he did in reviewing my book *The Design Revolution* for the February 2005 issue of *Back to*

Genesis (his review was titled "The Design Revelation"). I want here to respond to some of his charges and to give my own view on the divergence between intelligent design and creationism.

> **Criticism 1**: Morris regards intelligent design as not faithful to the full Christian revelation. For instance, he is concerned that "many Christians now seem to think that [the intelligent design movement] has freed them from having to confront the Genesis record of a young earth and global flood." He sees intelligent design's focus on an unspecified de-signer—indeed, a designer who need not even be a theistic creator God—as disingenuous and a matter of expedience, done simply "to build a very large tent, allowing anyone except pure materialists to take refuge there." Moreover, he implies that intelligent design advocates are guilty of snobbery, stating that "ID advocates would be embarrassed" to be associated with young earth creationism's "Biblical literalism."

> **Response 1**: Morris fails to address the fundamental issue here, namely, what is the proper scope of design-theoretic reasoning. In inferring design from aspects of the world, we are always looking at finite arrangements of material objects and events involving them. There is no way, logically speaking, to infer from such objects to an infinite, personal creator God. Thomas Aquinas understood this. Kant understood this. That's why intelligent design is not a biblical or religious doctrine. Morris is right that anyone except pure materialists can take refuge with intelligent design. This, however, should not be regarded as a bad thing. Creationism is a package deal, with a particular interpretation of Bible being part of the total package. Intelligent design, by contrast, is a partial truth, not the whole truth.

Morris, however, thinks that stressing this partial truth does disservice to the Christian faith. According to him, intelligent design is freeing Christians from having to confront the Genesis record of a young earth and global flood. But if Christians are ignoring Genesis, that's not a problem with intelligent design but with Christians not devoting sufficient care to biblical studies. Christians have an obligation to confront the Genesis record. But having confronted that record, must they end up where Morris and his colleagues end up? In particular, does confronting the Genesis record require interpreting it as teaching a young earth and a global flood?

Let me concede that young earth creationism was the position of the church from the Church Fathers through the Reformers. Yet, during that time, church teaching also held that the earth was stationary. Psalm 93 states that the earth is established forever and cannot be moved. A literal interpretation of Psalm 93 seems to require geocentrism. And yet everyone at the Institute for Creation Research (ICR) accepts the Copernican Revolution. Moreover, if literalism is the key to biblical hermeneutics, what are we to make of the seventh day of creation, the day of God's rest? Was it too a literal twenty-four hours in length? Many biblical scholars think that we are still in the seventh day.

This is well-worn ground, and young earth creationists have answers to these questions, just as those who interpret Genesis more figuratively have rebuttals. As Christians we have an obligation, as the Apostle Paul put it, to "rightly divide" (i.e., interpret) the Word of God. But what informs our interpretation of the Word? Clearly, our knowledge of the world plays some role. Our knowledge of physics from the 17th century on has made geocentrism no longer a viable option. In trying to balance the science of the day with the interpretation of Scripture, I therefore often come back to an observation of Charles Hodge. Early in his systematic theology, he noted that even though the Word of God is inerrant, our interpretations of it need not be; as a consequence, it can be a trial for the church when long-held interpretations are thrown into question.

Are Christians who advocate intelligent design being less than faithful to Christianity? Are we embarrassed to be associated with Biblical literalism? These questions are beside the point. Christians of many stripes are ID advocates, including biblical literalists who hold to a young earth. Non-Christians, too, are ID advocates. Biblical literalism is simply not an issue for intelligent design because the problem of explaining biological complexity holds independently of the age of the earth or one's interpretation of Genesis. Moreover, no one in the ID movement claims that ID is the Gospel. If you want the Gospel, read the Bible and especially the New Testament.

ID is part of God's general revelation. Consequently, it can be understood apart from the Bible. That's why, for instance, the Oxford Centre for Hindu Studies invited me to lecture on intelligent design and warmly embraced my message (this happened in October 2003). Just about anyone who is not wedded to a pure materialism agrees that some sort of design or purpose underlies nature. Intelligent design not only gives a voice to these people, but also gives them the tools to dismantle materialism.

Dismantling materialism is a good thing. Not only does intelligent design rid us of this ideology, which suffocates the human spirit, but, in my personal experience, I've found that it opens the path for people to come to Christ. Indeed, once materialism is no longer an option, Christianity again becomes an option. True, there are then also other options. But Christianity is more than able to hold its own once it is seen as a live option. The problem with materialism is that it rules out Christianity so completely that it is not even a live option. Thus, in its relation to Christianity, intelligent design should be viewed as a ground-clearing operation that gets rid of the intellectual rubbish that for generations has kept Christianity from receiving serious consideration.

Criticism 2: Morris claims that intelligent design brings nothing new to the debate: "It is not really a new approach, using basically the same evidence and arguments used for years by scientific creationists but made to appear more sophisticated with complex nomenclature and argumentation." Morris notes that the bacterial flagellum, the icon of intelligent design, was used by the late Dick Bliss. So too, my use of the term "specified complexity" as a criterion for detecting design has, according to Morris, "essentially the same meaning as 'organized complexity,' which is more meaningful and which I have often used myself." And as for my universal probability bound of $10^{(-150)}$, below which chance is precluded, Emile Borel proposed a less conservative one of $10^{(-50)}$ and Morris himself proposed a bound of $10^{(-110)}$.

Response 2: The debate between intelligent design and materialistic evolution is as old as civilization. Indeed, we can see this debate as far back as the ancient creation stories, some of which gave primacy to material forces and others of which gave primacy to intelligence (contrast the Babylonian with the

Memphite creation stories; the former appealed to material forces, the latter to creative intelligence). We see it also at the dawn of western philosophy, in which Greek atomistic philosophers like Democritus, Leucippus, and later Epicurus, championed a materialistic evolutionary process, whereas others, such as Anaxagoras, Plato, and the Stoics, argued for an intrinsic intelligence or purposiveness underlying the material world. The current controversy over materialistic theories of evolution and intelligent design is the latest incarnation of this debate.

At issue in Morris's criticism, therefore, is what have been the relative contributions of scientific creationism and intelligent design to this debate. My own view is that Morris at once overstates creationism's contributions here and understates those of intelligent design. Take Morris's notion of "organized complexity." The concept attempts to grasp something that is beyond the remit of purely material factors and could only result from a designing intelligence. But how are we to give rigor to this concept? Does, for instance, a river, as it carves out a convoluted path, constitute an instance of organized complexity? And if not, why not?

The problem with creationism's approach to design detection and ruling out chance is that its relevant concepts (like "organized complexity") were never developed beyond the intuitive, pretheoretic level (and this is true even of A. E. Wilder-Smith's ideas about information). Morris confirms this charge near the close of his book review: "A school child can easily tell a rounded stone from a crafted arrowhead—one shaped by natural forces, the other by skilled human hands. Just so, the incredible organized complexity of even the simplest one-celled organism speaks clearly of intelligent design, and one should not need sophisticated rhetoric or math to recognize this."

But that's just the problem: the logic of design detection is not perspicuous and, at the hands of creationists, was never developed with sufficient rigor. Evolutionary biologists look at a cell and see the effects of material mechanisms, most notably natural selection and random variation. If Morris wants simply to say that these scientists are being willfully ignorant, instances of those who suppress the truth as in Romans 1, then there is no point even in introducing a concept like "organized complexity." In that case, Morris should simply say that the design in creation is self-evident. End of story.

By contrast, much of my own work on intelligent design has been filling in the details of these otherwise intuitive, pretheoretic ideas of creationists. For instance, I learned about Emile Borel and his universal probability bound of $10^{(-50)}$ through the writings of the creationists. Indeed, I recall as an undergraduate reading on the Chicago subway a book by ICR associates Clifford Wilson and John Weldon debunking UFOs. That book had an appendix that examined the chance formation of the origin of life and mentioned Borel's universal probability bound.

Nonetheless, I found the probabilistic reasoning in the creationist literature incomplete and imprecise. For instance, authors often referred to the probability of the chance formation of a particular protein, but failed to note that the relevant probability was that of any protein that performed the same function (this is a much more difficult probability to calculate, and one with which recent ID research has been having some success). Another problem was taking the small probability of events as sufficient reason to rule out their chance occurrence without acknowledging that small probability by itself is not enough to rule out chance. What else is needed? In my theory of design detection, I argue that what's needed is a specification, that is, a type of pattern with certain mathematical and logical characteristics.

Hence, within my scheme, "specified complexity" or "specified improbability" becomes the key to identifying intelligence. This concept, however, is rigorously developed, as evidenced by the fact that my book on design detection was published as a research monograph with a mainstream academic publisher (*The Design Inference*, Cambridge University Press, in their series *Cambridge Studies in Probability, Induction, and Decision Theory*—note that I cite the Wilson and Weldon book here). Morris's concept or organized complexity, by contrast, was never rigorously developed and is the reason that, to this day, it has no traction within the scientific community.

There is an irony in Morris claiming that intelligent design brings nothing new to the table. Intelligent design is turning the study of design in nature into a bona fide science. By contrast, making design into a science has rarely been a priority for creationism. A. E. Wilder-Smith's work constitutes an exception, though without the relevant technical expertise, he was not in a position to develop his ideas rigorously. Moreover, I remember in the late 1980s him complaining to me that ICR would no longer publish his books. Instead of emphasizing and developing work pertinent to design, creationists have tended to focus on other issues, such as dating the earth or accounting for geology in terms of a global flood.

To be sure, creationists have made arguments from complexity that attempt to demonstrate the incapacity of material factors to bring about biological forms. But they have also argued that neither creation nor evolution are scientific at all because no one was there at the key origination events in the history of life to observe what really happened. Moreover, creationists have at times explicitly identified design as an intuitive idea not subject to rigorous scientific formulation (cf. the 1998 edition of Junker and Scherer's creationist biology text *Evolution: Ein Kritisches Lehrbuch*, which toward the end of the book makes precisely this point). The bottom line is that intelligent design is methodically developing a line of research about which creationism has been ambivalent.

I've focused here on my own contributions to ID. But the work of my ID colleagues falls in this same pattern of, on the one hand, refurbishing old ideas and, on the other, charting new research paths. Morris aptly notes that Dick Bliss used the bacterial flagellum "in his talks on creation a generation ago." Yet, for an analysis of the probabilistic hurdles involved in trying to evolve the protein parts of a flagellum by purely materialistic means so that the parts properly mesh (i.e., so that their interfaces are compatible, which is a necessary condition for the parts to work together to form a functioning protein machine), you will need to look to the ID literature and, specifically, to a 2004 article in *Protein Science* by Michael Behe and David Snoke.

ID has pushed the concept of design considerably further than creationism. This is reflected in the ID publication record, which includes books with mainstream trade presses, monographs with mainstream academic publishers, and peer-reviewed articles in mainstream scientific journals. The same cannot be said for creationism. True, there are creationist scientists with stellar academic credentials and scientific careers (e.g., Raymond Damadian, who invented the MRI). But they have made their reputations by doing work that does not explicitly argue for creation or design. My colleagues in the intelligent design movement, by contrast, are explicitly arguing for intelligent design in the mainstream academic and scientific literature.

Criticism 3: Finally, I want to take up Morris's concern that ID is, as he puts it, "ineffective." According to him, it is "no more convincing to evolutionists than is young-earth creationism." Here he cites Eugenie Scott, Ken Miller, and Howard Van Till as scientists who remain "unimpressed" by intelligent design.

Response 3: If the criterion for intelligent design's success were whether it is accepted by people like Scott, Miller, and Van Till, then Morris's concern would have merit. But that is not the criterion for its success. ID's criterion for success is rather the following: whether its arguments are sound, whether its evidence for design is solid, whether its critique of materialistic accounts of evolution holds up, whether it is developing into a fruitful scientific research program, and whether it is convincing to people with no stake in the outcome of this debate. On all these points, ID is proving quite effective.

To see this, ask yourself why the hard-core opponents of ID, who Morris claims are "unimpressed" with intelligent design, nonetheless spend an inordinate amount of time and effort trying to debunk it. Entire books in mainstream academic presses have now been written to debunk intelligent design (Forrest and Gross's *Creationism's Trojan Horse: The Wedge of Intelligent Design*, published by Oxford University Press, is just one example). The same cannot be said for creationism.

It's been said that the worst humiliation is not to be taken seriously. Despite their dismissive rhetoric, critics of ID are taking it seriously, and not just as a cultural force. Our scientific arguments are being challenged in the scientific literature. Critics may say that they are unimpressed, and, in their heart of hearts, they may feel that ID truly is nonsense. But it is pernicious nonsense. And like a hydra, it seems to keep growing new heads faster than the critics can lop them off.

Thomas Kuhn, in his *Structure of Scientific Revolutions*, clearly taught us that the old guard is not going to change its mind. By being wedded to a failing paradigm, they suffer from the misconceptions, blindspots, and prejudices that invariably accrue to a dying system of thought. Intelligent design is forcefully pointing up those failures.

Thus, to determine ID's effectiveness, the people to watch are those in the middle, who are viewing the debate and trying to figure out what side they should come down on. Increasingly, I'm finding that they are impressed with ID as they never were with creationism. Take, for instance, the well-known former atheist Antony Flew, whose conversion to theism (albeit a weak form of it) recently made international news. What did Flew cite as a key factor in his conversion? Not creationism but rather design-theoretic arguments for the intelligent origin of life.

By limiting itself to the design question and not getting distracted with the Bible-science controversy, ID is engaging the culture in ways that creationism never could. Young earth creationists have tended to operate in well-insulated enclaves. True, they have been the butt of much ridicule and attack from the outside, but by having their own schools and publishing houses, they have tended to be well-supported internally. Design theorists, by contrast, have squarely confronted the cultural mainstream (scientific, academic, and media). ID's voice is heard in places where young earth creationism is ignored.

But cultural engagement has come with a cost. Because ID advocates are unwilling to push design farther than its logic will go, we receive criticism from young earth creationists (Morris's criticism in his review of my book is mild by comparison with Ken Ham's). At the same time, the scientific and academic establishment has spared no effort to undermine, derail, and in some cases ruin the careers and efforts of ID advocates (my own case at Baylor has been widely publicized; I can provide details of numerous other cases; the fallout from the article by Stephen Meyer that appeared in the *Proceedings of the Biological Society of Washington* is the most recent case in point).

The Bible warns us to take heed if everyone is speaking well of us. In that case, ID advocates may have even less to worry about than young earth creationists.

I close with a story about Henry Morris's son John Morris, the president of ICR. In the spring of 2001, I was invited to give some talks at UCSD [University of California, San Diego] and in the surrounding area. John showed up at one of my talks, introduced himself, and invited me to visit him at the ICR campus. I took him up on his offer and visited the following day. He graciously showed me around and had me speak about intelligent design to the ICR scholars who were present that day (unfortunately, neither Henry Morris nor Duane Gish were in). Toward the end of my visit, John noted that ID fell short of a full creation model, but then commended ID for conclusively showing the bankruptcy of Darwinism. He was right. As a limited tool for dislodging materialism, developing the concept of design, and applying it to biological systems, ID is the best thing going. I would therefore like to encourage Henry Morris and all young-earth creationists to view intelligent design as a friend in the destruction of Darwinian materialism and in developing the scientific understanding of design in nature.

Morris's Letter to Dembski[1]

February 7, 2005

Dear Dr. Dembski,

My son, Dr. John Morris, has given me a copy of your concerned and thoughtful letter of February 1st. I am honored that you would respond to my review of your recent book with a response of your own, and I do hope we may have an opportunity to meet one of these days for an informal discussion on matters of mutual concern. As you say, we have too many common interests not to be supporting each other.

I do appreciate the valuable work being done by you and other I.D. writers, and I think the way you have been treated at Baylor (a once Baptist university!) is deplorable.[2] The recent actions against Richard Sternberg in relation to his publication of Stephen Meyer's article were even worse, but are understandable in view of the immovable mindset of the present scientific establishment. Total atheistic naturalism is their religion, and they will not be convinced otherwise by scientific arguments, no matter how compelling and sophisticated. One man admitted to me once, following a debate, that the scientific evidence really favored creation, but *science required* him to be committed to naturalism. During our more than 300 scientific debates on university campuses, we ICR scientists have seen many students turn from evolution to creation (some following later by becoming Christians) but *never* has one of our debate opponents changed his belief in evolution. That is probably true in your debates as well.

---

[1] Used by permission of Dr. John Morris.

[2] Editor's note: Morris is here referring to the firing of Dembski as head of the Michael Polanyi Center for Complexity, Information, and Design at Baylor University in Waco, Texas in 2000. See Tony Carnes, "Intelligent Design: Design Interference," *Christianity Today*, December 4, 2000, 20.

I might suggest that we who are called young earth creationists (that name must have been given us by the "progressive" creationists; I don't like it myself) would respond more favorably to the intelligent design advocates (we also believe strongly in intelligent design) if they would indicate they were really strengthening, instead of replacing, our foundational position. Instead, especially in your new book, you have gone out of your way to distance yourself from us. It does seem to us that you and others try to give the impression that your academic credentials are superior to ours, so that you can get a hearing in the academic world that we cannot.

That may be true to some degree, but you need to know that we have also spoken on hundreds of university campuses in this country, not to mention at least 25 other countries and on all continents. Hundreds of books and articles have been published trying (unsuccessfully, we think) to rebut our scientific arguments and we believe we have "won" all our 300+ debates, even though we never use Biblical arguments. As you know, Eugenie Scott has counseled her evolutionist colleagues never to debate a creationist, because they would probably "lose."

As far as "credentials" are concerned, Duane Gish has a PhD from Berkeley in biochemistry, Ken Cumming (our biology head) a PhD in genetics and ecology from Harvard, Steve Austin (our geology head) a PhD from Colorado State in Atmospheric Physics, etc. Mine is from the University of Minnesota. All of us have many publications in our own fields. My own senior/graduate level textbook in hydraulics and hydrology has been adopted in over 100 colleges and I was head of civil engineering at Virginia Tech for well over a decade. There are *many* other "young-earth creationists" with excellent academic credentials.

As far as your contention that intelligent design has a research potential not offered by scientific creationism, most of our M.S. graduates have produced worthwhile research related to their scientific fields as well as to creationism. Our RATE committee for eight years has been working on age-dating research and has come up with what seems like compelling radioactive evidences for recent creation. The Creation Research Society has been publishing worthwhile research articles for forty years. Admittedly this is largely rejected or ignored by the evolutionary establishment but this is still largely true of I.D. research as well.

As mentioned in my review, our experience (I have been in this arena for almost sixty years) has indicated that the so-called "wedge" strategy is futile. Neither one of our two approaches will convince the Eugenie Scotts of academia, not to mention the likes of Richard Dawkins. When we began ICR back in 1970, we did try the "wedge" approach for a while. For example, our textbook, *Scientific Creationism* was also issued in a Public School Edition, with no religious material, but it soon went out of print. In the meantime, the General Edition has been used to win many evolutionists to creationism. Many of these "converts," like myself, had believed in evolution for what they assumed were compelling scientific proofs even though they would have rather believed in creationism for personal reasons. They often express a sense of gratified relief when they suddenly find out that they can be "intellectually fulfilled Bible-believing creationists" (apologies to R. Dawkins!).

You tend to minimalize literal six-day creationism as merely one possible interpretation of Genesis, which you reject because of the age issue. This is exactly why we insist that the geological data are at least as important as biological in dealing with origins. Most evolutionists will remain committed to Darwinism, regardless of design complexity problems, as long as they believe in the geological ages. "Time is the hero," as George Wald said. Yet most I.D. writers accept the billion-year history of life, which is the only real basis of evolutionism. This means they must ignore what to us is the determinative issue of suffering and death before sin. The alleged scientific problems of flood geology and age dating are insignificant, in our judgment, compared to the theological and Biblical problems posed by that issue. That is why much of our creationist research has focused on physical rather than biological questions (although the GENE committee and other creationist biologists have already shown the genetic impossibility of "vertical" evolution).

We also are convinced (although this is not a question of salvation or Christian fellowship) that the literal six-day creation of all things is not merely an option, but the *only* teaching of origins sanctioned by Scripture in general and the Lord Jesus in particular (note Mark 10:6 for example). No one yet has really answered our evidence on this factor, though Hugh Ross and others have equivocated with them. In the book *Biblical Creationism*, I have analyzed and expounded upon every passage in the Bible mentioning creation, the Flood or related topics—with the conclusion that there is not even a hint anywhere in Scripture suggesting evolution or the long ages that would be required for evolution. We believe that Christians should not dismiss such Biblical arguments and authority out of hand. In particular the idea of a billion years or more of pre-human hominid death makes God to be a sadist and the Gospel redundant (death cannot be the wages of sin, but the pleasure of God).

When I first became a creationist back about 1944 (through studying both Scripture and the evolutionary literature; there was very little sound creationist literature at that time), I was teaching at Rice and was trying to witness to the students there, almost all of whom had been sent there by the Navy to study science and engineering. During those early years I could find or learn about very few, if any, university professors or practicing scientists who were creationists, or even Bible-believing Christians. Now there are many of them everywhere, most of them having become scientific creationists largely as a result of our literature. I can't help but wonder why you feel the evidence in our books and articles is so unconvincing (I alone have written some sixty books, not to mention those by many others; have you ever really *studied* any of these yourself, besides those of Wilder-Smith, who by the way, had himself been greatly influenced by *The Genesis Flood*?). Admittedly our scientific creationism books have not convinced the die-hard evolutionists—but neither have the I.D. books. The widely publicized case of Anthony Flew changing from atheism to semi-deism is worth noting, of course, as a rare exception. I might mention Dean Kenyon as one of our own important "converts."

I need to note one or two other minor points in your response. You said Dr. Wilder-Smith complained that ICR stopped publishing his books. He may have misunderstood the situation. Creation-Life Publishers not (ICR) did publish several of his books, and I assume they had to stop for financial reasons. We had nothing to do with this, but I do know that CLP lost money right from the start—including on his books. They finally had to sell out to avoid bankruptcy. I am sure any such decision (if it ever really happened) was not because of any scientific or doctrinal disagreement. Most of his books would probably never have been published at all, except for my recommendation to CLP.

Although you are right in noting that creationism is most influential here in the United States, it is true that it is now growing in many other nations, especially in Korea, England, Australia and Canada. There are also small but growing organizations in Japan, Russia, Sweden, Germany and probably a dozen or more others. Most of these were started in part as a result of the ICR ministries. The South Korean Association, for example (organized in 1980 by Dr. Gish and myself), now claims hundreds of scientists, has published many books, and even organized a college.

We have never made creationism a "package deal" as you call it, requiring belief in Genesis. In particular, we never have advocated Biblical creationism for public schools—but only the scientific evidences both pro and con for both evolution and creation. We definitely do not want non-Christian teachers to be compelled to teach Biblical creationism (or Christianity in general) in public schools. We have always advised against legislation or litigation to promote creation. The various laws that have been attempted—in Louisiana and Arkansas, for example—were neither proposed nor sponsored by the ICR, but these laws were also clearly secular. Nevertheless the courts insisted they were "religious," just as evolutionists are now reacting against the I.D.

As far as teaching about the Flood and the age of the earth are concerned, there are many strong scientific arguments for these that would be legitimate topics for discussion in geology, physics or history classes; however since these are also Biblical topics, secularists insist they are off-limits, and we have never pushed them for public schools. In fact, we think Christians should send their children to Christian schools (or home schools) where these certainly are appropriate topics to include in their curricula. At ICR we have two sets of "tenets of Creationism"—one scientific and one Biblical. They are consistent with each other, but each can also be taught independently of the other.

We at ICR do accept the Copernican revolution, as you say, but we also recognize that some creationists can make impressive arguments for geocentricism. My own belief (not necessarily that of others, even at ICR) is that the universe is essentially infinite in size, and therefore it is not even possible to define its center. At any rate, it is not something to insist on, as some modern geocentricists are trying to do.

I think you are wrong in saying that our reasonings in terms of probability are "sloppy." Yours are surely more sophisticated (and therefore will not be understandable to most) but ours do make the point—not only mine, but those of Wilder-Smith, Coppedge and others.

We are certainly appalled by the attempts of the academic establishment to undermine the careers of some I.D. advocates. We have been down that same road often ourselves. You might read Jerry Bergman's book *The Criterion* on that subject, for many examples. I have taught at five secular universities myself, encountering similar opposition at each one. At Virginia Tech, for example, faculty delegations twice attempted to have the president remove me from my department chairmanship. They were unsuccessful, however, because my department was exemplary and my own personal record was good.

Finally, let me repeat what I said earlier. We do appreciate the significant contributions made by I.D. advocates to the venerable design argument. If these were presented simply in that context, and not as a substitute for scientific creationism, we would be completely positive about it. Neither can ever be the final answer, because the battle is basically spiritual (my book *The Long War Against God* has documented the age-long worldwide warfare of Satan against our Creator and His purpose in creation) and can only be ultimately resolved in that arena. Ultimate victory depends on God, so we dare not distort His Word and His character just to appeal to secular scientism.

I certainly do hope we can meet some day, although at my age (86.4) and with my wife's 4.5 year battle with Alzheimer's) this may have to be in Paradise!

With best wishes and regards.

Sincerely in Christ,

Henry M. Morris
President Emeritus

Appendix E

CMI's Views on the Intelligent Design Movement[1]

Carl Wieland

30 August 2002

Introduction

The argument of 'intelligent design' (ID) has a long history going back to the ancient Greeks and Romans.[2] It was persuasively articulated by William Paley (1743–1805), who put forward the argument of an inferred divine Watchmaker in his book *Natural Theology* (1802). Modern biblical creationists have also used the design argument in their opposition to evolution.[3] But the works of modern scholars such as Michael Denton (*Evolution: A Theory in Crisis*, 1985) and Phillip Johnson (*Darwin on Trial*, 1991) have led to the formation of an association of scientists and other scholars, which has become known as the 'Intelligent Design Movement' (IDM or ID movement).

---

[1] This article is the position statement on the Intelligent Design Movement by the prominent creation organization Creation Ministries International. It was originally published in 2002 and can be found on the organization's website (creation.com). It is reprinted here by permission of CMI.

[2] Cicero, for example, used design in support of the Greek pantheon of gods. See also "A brief history of design," http://creation.com/a-brief-history-of-design.

[3] A.E. Wilder-Smith, *The Creation of Life* (Wheaton: Harold Shaw, 1970), Robert Kofahl and Kelly Segraves, *The Creation Explanation* (Wheaton: Harold Shaw, 1975) and Henry Morris and Gary Parker, *What Is Creation Science?* (El Cajon: Master Books, 1982).

Many of our supporters have asked us repeatedly for our position on the IDM, so this document is in response to that. It is not intended to be a hostile review by any means. Many in the creation movement, including me personally, have friendly relations with, and personally like, some of the people prominent in the IDM.

The modern concept of intelligent design has been simply formulated as the belief that certain biological lines of evidence (e.g., the 'irreducible complexity' of features such as the bacterial flagellum) are evidence for a designer and against blind naturalistic processes.

The Modern Intelligent Design Movement (IDM)

The Intelligent Design Movement's motivation appears to be the desire to challenge the blind acceptance of the materialistic, godless, naturalistic philosophy of Darwinian evolution. They confront many of the philosophical underpinnings of today's evolutionary thinking. As a movement, they are unwilling to align themselves with biblical creationism.

The informal leadership of the IDM has more or less come to rest on Phillip Johnson, a distinguished retired (emeritus) Professor of Law at the University of California at Berkeley who is a Presbyterian. Philosophically and theologically, the leading lights of the ID movement form an eclectic group. For example, Dr Jonathan Wells is not only a scientist but also an ordained cleric in the Unification Church (the 'Moonie' sect) and Dr Michael Denton is a former agnostic anti-evolutionist (with respect to biological transformism), who now professes a vague form of theism. However, he now seems to have embraced evolutionary (though somehow 'guided') transformism. Dr Michael Behe, author of *Darwin's Black Box*, is a Roman Catholic who says he has no problem with the idea that all organisms, including man, descended from a common ancestor.

The IDM's General Approach

Among the IDM's leading proponents, there are some commonly shared beliefs and stances:

- The major focus of their attacks is not evolution as such, but 'chance' evolution, i.e., the naturalistic philosophy (there is no supernatural; matter is all there is) behind it.

- Anyone opposed to naturalism could potentially qualify as an ally. This includes believers in evolution from microbe to man, so long as this belief were to involve some intelligent, planned interference sometime during the billions of years.

- They generally believe in, or are publicly neutral on, the millions and billions of years that evolutionists teach and accept.

- They either are comfortable with, or express no public view on, the corollary implication of long-age belief, namely that millions of years of death, disease and suffering took place before mankind appeared.

- Though the movement incorporates some believers in Genesis, including recent creation in six days and Noah's global Flood, its approach would preclude public expression of support or concern for the Bible's authority in such matters.

- They often go to great lengths to ensure that they are not seen as 'coming at it from the Bible'.

The concept of the ID movement has attracted a number of evangelical Christians, including believers in literal Genesis, who see it as a helpful new strategy to crack the foundation of evolution, which undergirds most of the world's cultures and schools.

Evidence of ID's growing activism was the effort to add the Santorum amendment to the 2002 US education bill (an amendment that encouraged schools to inform students about the 'continuing controversy' over 'biological evolution'). ID leaders have also been active in ongoing efforts to include ID in the educational standards of the US state of Ohio.

The IDM's Perceived and Potential Strengths

- Many biblical (or Genesis) creationists (BCs, who by histori- cally sound exegetical standards are convinced of recent crea- tion) realize that the IDM 'doesn't go as far as we like', but think that this is a reasonable price to pay for what they see as a potentially effective 'thin edge of the wedge' strategy. They reason, 'Let's just get the camel's nose inside the tent, then we can concentrate on these other issues. Let's win one battle at a time.'

- IDM sympathizers among BCs, frustrated by the failed leg- islative attempts to force the teaching of 'two models', generally think that this tactic has a better chance of getting them a hearing in the social/legislative arena. (CMI has never supported *compulsion* to teach creation, by the way, and does not support the artificial separation into the categories of 'scientific' vs 'biblical' creationism that characterized much of the 'two-model approach.') They probably believe that this is because:

  - They can tap into the intellectual, academic and political clout of a greater range of people than just Bible-believ- ing Christians.

  - By having non-Christians in the movement, it will ap- pear less parochial and 'biased'.

  - By 'keeping the Bible out of it', they likely believe that this will overcome the 'separation of church and state' interpretations of the US Constitution that have pre- vailed in recent years. They would therefore be inclined to argue that this is a 'tactical necessity'.

- The movement's apparent refusal to identify the hypo-thetical designer with the biblical God (some IDers have pointed out that the design work they postulate could even have been performed by aliens) is seen as a prudent necessity to keep the argument on philosophically 'neu-tral' ground, and thus avoid a lot of anti-Christian hos-tility.

CMI's Perception of the Positives of the IDM

- It has produced some materials and arguments which, though not necessarily designed to help the battle for biblical creation, have been very useful in this cause.

- It has kept the anti-creationists occupied on another flank of the battle, i.e., it has drawn some of the fire which might oth-erwise have distracted us from allocating our full efforts to spreading our message.

- It correctly draws attention to the fact that the teaching of Darwinism is not philosophically/religiously neutral, but is squarely based upon the presuppositions of naturalism (an-other word for philosophical materialism or atheism, i.e., that there is no supernatural, but that this material world is all there is).

CMI's Perception of IDM's Weaknesses

- Despite incorporating some extremely bright thinkers, the movement as a whole seems to have a recurring philosophical blind spot. Though they often correctly point out the religious foundations of Darwinism, the fact that all scientific reasoning is ultimately based on axioms/presuppositions (which are un-provable, hence metaphysical/subjective/biased by definition) should have alerted them to the fact that there is no such thing as a 'neutral' scientific arena within which to interpret the evidence related to the past.

- Since the only thing in their platform which comes close to being a commonly shared presupposition is a negative (naturalism is wrong), they can provide no coherent philosophical framework on which to base the axioms necessary to interpret evidence relevant to the historical sciences (paleontology, historical geology, etc). So they can never offer a 'story of the past', which is one more reason why they must continually limit the debate to one of mechanism—and then only in broad, general terms (designed vs undesigned).

- They generally refuse to be drawn on the sequence of events, or the exact history of life on Earth or its duration, apart from saying, in effect, that it 'doesn't matter'. However, this is seen by the average evolutionist as either absurd or disingenuously evasive—the arena in which they are seeking to be regarded as full players is one which directly involves historical issues. In other words, if the origins debate is not about a 'story of the past', what is it about?

- Their failure to identify themselves with a story of the past (e.g. Genesis) is partly tactically driven, but is also a necessity, because they do not agree within themselves on a story of the past. However, this failure only reinforces the perception by the establishment that they are really 'creationists in disguise'. The attacks on the IDM have thus been virtually as ferocious as any on Genesis creationists. Thus, the belief that agreeing to 'keep the Bible out of it' would serve to keep antireligious hostility out of the arena has not been confirmed in practice.

- Some who are prominent in the IDM appear to be sympathetic to the Bible's account of Creation. However, if the movement should ever make the strategic inroads it hopes for, then our concern would be that any of its leaders who might later identify themselves with Genesis belief would lay themselves open to charges of having been publicly deceptive.

Ironically, despite already drawing the fire aimed at Genesis, the Bible and Christianity, many other prominent figures in the IDM reject or are hostile to biblical creation, especially the notion of the recent creation of a good world, ruined by man's Fall into sin. For tactical reasons, they have been urged (especially by their coolest and wisest head, Phil Johnson, who does not himself share that hostility) not to publicly condemn their Genesis-believing fellow travelers, although this simmering opposition has burst forth from time to time. Were the IDM to partially succeed in its initial aims, some of the strongest opponents of literal Genesis may well arise from its recently victorious ranks. For instance, Dr Michael Denton, though an amiable fellow, was nevertheless part of a broadcast forum in Australia which recently told a largely Christian audience that belief in literal Genesis was foolish and unscientific.

- The IDM's refusal to identify the Designer with the biblical God, and in particular with the *history* in the Bible, means that:

  - Acceptance of ID thinking *en masse* could just as easily lead to New-Age or Hindu-like notions of creation, as well as weird alien sci-fi notions.[4] In such instances, a Christian might well see that the metaphorical exorcism of one socio-philosophical demon would have achieved merely its replacement by others, possibly worse.

  - There is no philosophical answer to their opponents' logically deduced charge that the Designer was monstrous and/or inept ('look at all the horrible, cruel, even defective things in the living world'), since bringing up the Fall is deliberately, tactically excluded. (However, the Fall was a major event in history, that changed every-

---

[4] See the 2004 book by CMI speaker Gary Bates: *Alien Intrusion: UFOs and the Evolution Connection* (Green Forest, AR: Master Books, 2004).

thing. The world we are looking at now is a world that has been corrupted by sin, not the original world that God designed). Thus, the movement's success could very likely even be counterproductive, by laying the biblical God open to ridicule and contempt in new ways.

In fact, these points are not just hypothetical. Historically, the 'intelligent design in isolation' argument has achieved just these sorts of negative results. In other words, it's been tried before and failed. The 'natural theology' approach (using design, but keeping the Bible out of it) by the deists of former centuries led to an increase in deistic belief, i.e. 'a different god' just as in the first point immediately above, with its attendant rejection of the Bible and the Gospel. The deists' driving force was the rejection of God's Word and, concomitantly, His right to exercise rule over our lives.

Urged to deduce the existence of the Creator God from 'design alone', and thus leaving out the Fall and the real history of the world, thinkers concluded that any creator God must be cruel, wasteful, etc. Charles Darwin himself wrote in exactly that vein. He also provided another example of the negative effects of leaving the biblical history out of the discussion. When he came across obvious examples of adaptive radiation from mainland populations onto islands, the only 'concept' of creation he had in his mind, in association with most of his deistically influenced scientist contemporaries, was *in situ* creation, which his observations spoke so strongly against. But of course if he had built into his thinking dispersal of all land vertebrates from one central point after the global Flood, the alleged problem would have vanished. So, intelligent design arguments that 'left the Bible out of it' actually aided and abetted, in a major way, the rising rejection of the Bible. Far from countering atheism, it actually pushed thinkers into a non-design explanation, hence further into naturalism and atheism.

This is not surprising. The Apostle Paul acknowledges the power of the design argument in Romans 1:20: God's eternal power and divine nature can be clearly understood from the things that have been made (i.e. evidence of design in nature). Because of this, the ungodly are 'without excuse.' But he maintains that people *willingly reject* this clear evidence. Peter likewise says in 2 Peter 3:3-6 that those who reject the supernatural Creation and the global Flood are 'willingly ignorant' (KJV) or 'deliberately forget[ful]' (NIV). Evidence of design in nature is enough to condemn men, but it is not enough to save them. The Bible makes it overwhelmingly clear that the scientific aspects of creation ministry cannot, in the end, be separated from the preaching of the Gospel, to enable people to be reconciled to their Creator. Deducing the details of creation from nature alone, unguided by His revealed Word, ignores the fact that nature is fallen and cursed. The great theologian Louis Berkhof wrote: '... since the entrance of sin into the world, man can gather true knowledge about God from His general revelation only if he studies it in the light of Scripture. ... '[5]

The IDM as a whole does not come to grips with the historical background of naturalism in the sciences. Biblical creationists have long argued that the millions-of-years concepts (which the majority of leading IDMers either support or say they have 'no problem with') in fields like astronomy/cosmology and historical geology were squarely based on, derived from, and fueled by, naturalism — i.e., the deliberate rejection of God's Word and its authority in relation to the history of the world.[6] These naturalism-underpinned

---

[5] Louis Berkhof, *Introductory Volume to Systematic Theology* (Grand Rapids: Eerdmans Publishing Co., 1938), 60.

[6] See two relevant articles by Dr Terry Mortenson on this point:

- 'Defining Boundaries on Creation and Noah's Flood: Early 19th Century British Scriptural Geologists,' which discusses these writers who perceived the then-developing old-Earth geology to be based on naturalism (order it free by email from Zondervan's Web site: www.zondervanchurchsource.com/convention) and

- "British scriptural geologists in the first half of the nineteenth century: part 2," http://creation.com/british-scriptural-geologists-in-the-first-half-of-the-nineteenth-century-part-2 (especially the section entitled 'The Philosophical Foundation of *Comparative Estimate*'),

conclusions of geology/astronomy were the seedbed for Darwinism. **That is, naturalism was there long before Darwinism and led directly to its dominance.** It is therefore ironic to observe IDers telling people that fighting 'naturalism' is the important issue, when at the same time they tell people that the very naturalism-based issues which were the seedbed of Darwinism are 'unimportant.'

Interestingly, a recent book produced from within the IDM, *Darwin's God* by Cornelius Hunter, argues powerfully that Darwin was really trying to distance God from natural evil, by removing Him from having anything to do with His creation. In other words, Darwin was in that sense an ultra-deist, rather than an atheist. Hunter shows how the problem is a particular view of God, of what He would or would not do. But indirectly, this would appear to argue against one aspect of the ID platform, since the only way to have a correct view of God and what He would do (and did do) would be if God revealed it to us, as indeed He has through Scripture. And Hunter's book often refers obliquely to biblical passages.

What About Public Education?

We tend to blame 'the world' for what has happened to our educational institutions. We don't usually stop to think of how the church itself has aided and abetted this tragedy as it has so often compromised on the authority of God's Word in relation to real-world issues such as science and history. CMI's major 'strategy' is to boldly, but humbly, call the church back to its biblical foundations in such matters, reforming the thinking of Christians, who are then to be salt and light to our culture. This is how it worked in the days of the Great Awakening in England and America, when the light of the Gospel diffused horizontally through the educational, political and social institutions, transforming positively just about everything we take for granted in our modern world.

---

which discusses the philosophically astute writings of one of the Scriptural geologists.

We have always felt that teachers should at least be able to critically examine arguments for and against evolution, and we don't think that the constitutional arguments in the USA supposedly preventing that have ever been strong, i.e., how can any Christian teacher who wants to do so be prevented from giving arguments for and against evolution? What reasonable person could logically defend the notion of shielding any scientific theory or idea from all critical analysis?

At the same time, we have never supported compulsory teaching of biblical creation (imagine any teacher being forced to teach that which they don't believe, and which in effect points the finger at them as sinners).

As indicated earlier, we also don't believe that one can, or should attempt to, artificially separate 'biblical' from 'scientific' creation in order to gain a hearing in the public arena. This has been attempted by biblical creationists, again for tactical reasons, with good motives. But, like the IDM's broader but ultimately similar stratagem, it appears to us to be philosophically flawed.

The origins issue has never been about facts and evidence as such—we all have the same world, the same evidence, the same facts. It is the philosophical framework within which facts are interpreted which differs. And philosophical frameworks are based on axioms (presuppositions, or starting beliefs). The scientific conclusions of Darwinism are squarely based on anti-biblical (naturalistic) axioms, while those of creation are based on biblical axioms. We believe that axioms need to be openly 'on the table', and it should be realized that one can discuss them in a secular setting without *teaching* religious doctrine as such, but without hiding or running away from the implications. The evidence concerning origins can be discussed through a critical comparison of axiom-based models[7] without fos-

---

[7] What about the common objection, 'Why not then teach e.g., Australian Aboriginal creation stories in science lessons?' One could ask such

tering the secular myth of 'neutrality,' i.e., that evidence 'speaks for itself' in some mysterious way.

What About the Constitutional Barriers?

US courts have consistently 'reinterpreted' the Constitution, and the US public mood has become increasingly secular. Why has this societal shift occurred? Because the church *en masse* has had its eyes shut to the foundational philosophical/worldview shift in Western culture. For this failure to adequately defend the authority of Genesis the church bears grave responsibility. Again, we see that the pressing need and priority is to reform the church in order to 're-salt' the culture; the legal/political battles will then become totally reframed. We fear that Christians who play 'let's pretend the Bible isn't part of it' risk alienating the culture still further.

Of course, in practical terms, starting with the powerful design arguments which the IDM has helped to reawaken (and has formalized in modern terms) can be a very useful tool for 'opening discussion', especially in circles where mentioning the Bible would instantly plug the hearer's ears. Many of us in CMI have actually been partially using the 'wedge' tactic of the IDM for years individually. That is, we may, in certain settings, seek to gain a more ready hearing through initially focusing on less controversial as-

---

objectors whether they are aware of any origins teaching outside of the Abrahamic stream which:

- Claims to be absolute revelational truth from the Creator in documentary form
- Has been held and believed consistently for many centuries in essentially its modern form.
- Has been held to offer a serious historical explanation for all of reality and the origins of man and the universe.
- Is supported by a significant group of qualified scientists and other intellectuals who are convinced that it does indeed explain the data at least as well as evolution/long ages.

pects of biblical creation. However, unlike the official stance of the IDM, when that opening comes, or when questioned, we will unhesitatingly affirm that we start our thinking based squarely on the real history in the Bible. Used properly, such a tactic is almost inevitably more effective than acting as if there is a neutral 'science' arena for determining truth. Most people get the point when one shows them how evidence is not neutral and does not speak for itself but must be interpreted. Even unbelievers are often willing to follow an argument when asked to temporarily alter their presuppositions (i.e., to 'put on a different pair of glasses') to see how the evidence might fit a biblical worldview. So, while it may be useful on occasion to focus on the evidence and avoid references to the Bible and religion, it is counterproductive if one does so to an extent that reinforces the myth that it is somehow less 'scientific' to base one's models on God's revelation, the Bible.

Summary and Conclusion

CMI supports the ID movement's efforts to promote academic freedom and to question evolution. When we call into question (hopefully with humility) aspects of their strategy, we do so not to seek to undermine or oppose their efforts, but to encourage careful thinking by all concerned believers (including ourselves) concerning the ways to achieve the most good, and to give most honor and glory to God. In the end, we in CMI are concerned about the truth and authority of the Word of God, the Bible. This is an issue which ultimately transcends and overrides matters such as local school politics and the like.

God, who used even the pagan king Cyrus for His purposes, may use the IDM in spite of the concerns we have raised. We would be delighted to see it make real inroads in the areas of its interest, and are positive about many aspects of its existence, including some of the useful materials it produces. Where we can be natural allies, if this can occur without compromising our biblical stance in any way, we want to be.

Our friends in the IDM will hopefully understand that when we discuss these problems and issues, we do so not to discourage or obstruct, but simply to make it clear where we are coming from, why we do so, and why we neither count ourselves a part of this movement nor campaign against it.

Appendix F

Is the Intelligent Design Movement Christian?[1]

Dr. Georgia Purdom

One player in the "war of the worldviews" is the intelligent design movement. ID has gained increasing recognition and publicity over the last several years at both local and national levels. It is especially well known in educational circles, where it has been heralded as an alternative to Darwinism/naturalism.

Intelligent design can be defined as a theory that holds that "certain features" of living things were designed by an "intelligent cause" as opposed to being formed through purely natural means.[2] The ID theory does not name the intelligent cause, and it does not claim that everything is designed, thus allowing for evolution/natural causes to play a role.

The historical roots of the ID movement lie in the natural theology movement of the 18th and 19th centuries. William Paley (1743–1805) reasoned that if one walked across a field and came upon a watch, the assumption would be that there had to be a watchmaker—the complexity and purpose of the watch points to the fact that it is not the result of undirected, unintelligent causes, but the product of a designer.[3] Natural theology sought to support the existence of God

---

[1] Taken from *The New Answers Book 2*, Ken Ham general editor, fifth printing, September 2009, pp. 135-41. Used with permission of Master Books, Green Forest, AR, 2008.

[2] Discovery Institute Center for Science and Culture, www.discovery.org/csc/topQuestions.php, September 13, 2005.

[3] W. Paley, *Paley's Watchmaker*, edited by Bill Cooper (West Sussex, England: New Wine Press, 1997, first published in 1802), 29–31.

through nature (general revelation) apart from the Bible (special revelation), since the Bible was facing much criticism at that time. The scientific knowledge of that time was grossly deficient, and it was thought that natural causes were sufficient to bring everything into existence.

In the last 100 years or so, there has been an explosion of knowledge about the complexity of cells, DNA, and microorganisms. Thus, the need for a designer has become even greater. The current ID movement has more than just philosophical arguments for a designer; it uses scientific evidence drawn from biology, chemistry, and physics.

Irreducible Complexity

The ID concept affirms that living things are designed and exhibit *irreducible complexity*. Some examples are the biochemistry of vision and the mammalian blood-clotting pathway. These biological pathways consist of many factors, and *all* the factors are necessary for the pathway to function properly. Thus, evolution (which works via the mechanism of small, gradual steps that keep only that which is immediately functional) could not have formed these pathways. For example, if only three of the blood-clotting factors (there are many factors in the complete pathway) were formed in an organism, blood would not clot, and thus the factors would not be kept because they are not currently useful to the organism. Evolutionary processes do not allow the organism to keep the three factors in the hopes that one day the rest of the blood-clotting factors will form. Evolution is goalless and purposeless; therefore, it does not keep the leftovers.

The question of whether a feature of a living organism displays design can be answered by using what is called an explanatory filter. The filter has three levels of explanation:

1. Necessity—did it have to happen?

2. Chance—did it happen by accident?

3. Design—did an intelligent agent cause it to happen?

This is a very logical, commonsense approach used by individuals every day to deduce cause and effect. For example, consider the scenario of a woman falling:

1. Did she have to fall? No, but she did.

2. Was it an accident?

3. Or was she pushed?

If we apply this explanatory filter to living organisms, a feature must be designed if the first two answers are no.

Let us evaluate the blood-clotting pathway with respect to these three questions:

1. The blood-clotting pathway is compatible with, but not required by, the natural laws of biology and chemistry; so it is not a necessity specified by natural phenomena.

2. It is complex because it is composed of many factors, thus the remote probability that it happened by chance. (Note that complex structures fall into two categories: ordered complexity and specified complexity. A snowflake, although complex structurally, has little information and thus is considered an example of ordered complexity. It is the direct result of natural phenomena rather than intelligent design[4]).

3. The blood-clotting pathway does show design, referred to as specified complexity, because it is complex and has a high amount of information. It is the direct result of an intelligent agent. All the factors must be present and interact with each other in a specified manner in order for the

---

[4] See www.intelligentdesign.org/menu/complex/complex3.htm for a more detailed discussion.

pathway to be functional. Thus, the blood-clotting pathway meets all the requirements for irreducible complexity, and so must be designed.

What the ID Movement Is and Is Not

William Dembski states, "ID is three things: a scientific research program that investigates the effects of intelligent causes; an intellectual movement that challenges Darwinism and its naturalistic legacy; and a way of understanding divine action."[5] The ID theory focuses on what is designed rather than answering the questions of who, when, why, and how. Those within the movement believe this promotes scientific endeavor by looking for function and purpose in those things that are designed, whereas an evolutionary mindset presupposes waste and purposelessness and aborts further scientific thinking. Although it may be a way of understanding divine action outside of a biblical framework, there are some serious implications for the Creator, which we will discuss later.

The ID movement does not speak to the optimality of design because it does not attempt to explain all designs. Remember, only "certain features" are designed, and evolutionary processes are not ruled out. The ID movement also claims not to be religiously motivated. It focuses not on the whom but on the what. This may sound very appealing at first glance. Some biblical creationists believe that the ID movement's tolerance and acceptance of a wide range of beliefs about the supernatural could be useful in reaching a larger audience. Since the movement is very careful not to associate itself with Christianity or any formal religion, some think it will stand a better chance of gaining acceptance as an alternative to Darwinism in the schools, because it does not violate the so-called separation of church and state.

The ID movement does have several positives. The movement has produced many resources, including books and multimedia, that

---

[5] W. Dembski, "Science and Design," *First Things* 86 (1998): 21–27.

support the biblical creationist viewpoint. It makes clear that Darwinism/naturalism is based on the presupposition that the supernatural does not exist, thus affecting the way one interprets the scientific evidence. ID is based on the presupposition that the supernatural does exist.

ID may serve as a useful tool in *preliminary* discussions about God and creation to gain an audience that might be turned off at the mention of the Bible. However, in further discussions, the Bible as the biblical creationists' foundation should be primary.[6]

The central problem with the ID movement is a divorce of the Creator from creation. The Creator and His creation cannot be separated; they reflect on each other. All other problems within the movement stem from this one.

Those within the ID movement claim their science is neutral. However, science is not neutral because it works with hypotheses based on beliefs or presuppositions. It is ironic that ID adherents refuse to see this about their own science, considering that they claim the problem with Darwinism is the presupposition that nothing supernatural exists. All scientists approach their work with presuppositions. The question is whether those beliefs are rooted in man's fallible ideas about the past or rooted in the infallible Word of God, the Bible.

The natural theology movement of the 1800s failed because it did not answer the next logical question: if it is designed, then who designed it? Although most within this movement claimed that design pointed to the God of the Bible, by divorcing general revelation (nature) from special revelation (the Bible), they opened the door to other conclusions. Deism (another movement of the same period) took the idea of excluding the Bible to the extreme and said God can

---

[6] See *AiG's views on the Intelligent Design Movement*, www.Answers InGenesis.org/ID.

only be known through nature and human reason, and that faith and revelation do not exist.

In today's culture, many are attracted to the ID movement because they can decide for themselves who the creator is—a Great Spirit, Brahman, Allah, God, etc. The current movement does not have unity on the naming of the creator and focuses more on what is designed. Thus, adherents do not oppose an old age for the earth and allow evolution to play a vital role once the designer formed the basics of life. They fail to understand that a belief in long ages for the earth formed the foundation of Darwinism. If God's Word is not true concerning the age of the earth, then maybe it's not true concerning other events of the creation week, and maybe God was not a necessary part of the equation for life after all.

The ID movement's belief in evolution also allows them to distance themselves from the problem of evil in the natural world. Examples of this include pathogenic microbes, carnivorous animals, disease, and death.

Without the framework of the Bible and the understanding that evil entered the world through man's actions (Genesis 3), God appears sloppy and incompetent, if not downright vicious. People ask why God is unable to prevent evil from thwarting His plans, resulting in such poor design, instead of understanding that because of the Fall there is now a "cursed" design. In addition, because the ID movement does not acknowledge God as Redeemer, there seems to be no final solution for the evil in this world, and by all appearances evil will continue to reign supreme. However, when we trust the Bible, we read that Jesus clearly conquered death by His Resurrection (Romans 6:3–10) and one day death will no longer reign (Revelation 21:4). Again, the Creator and His creation cannot be separated.

The attributes of God are very important when resolving apparent discrepancies in His creation. For example, according to the Bible, the earth is around 6,000 years old. However, starlight can be seen from stars millions of light years away. Also, according to the Bible,

God does not lie. Therefore, we must lack some information that would resolve this apparent discrepancy. (Some good research has been done on this issue, and there are several plausible solutions.[7])

Our Creator and Redeemer

Romans 1:20 states that all men know about God through His creation. However, just recognizing that there is a designer is only the first step. Colossians 1:15–20 and 2 Peter 3:3–6 point to the inexorable link between God's role as Creator *and* Redeemer. In Colossians, Paul talks about God as Creator and moves seamlessly to His role as Redeemer. Paul sees creation as a foundation for redemption. In 1 Peter, Peter states that people started disbelieving in the second coming of Christ because they started doubting God's role as Creator. Again, God's role as Creator becomes foundational to His role as Redeemer. Recognizing a designer is not enough to be saved; submitting to the Redeemer is also necessary. While some might consider ID to be a noble attempt to counter the evolutionary indoctrination of our culture, it falls far short of a thoroughly biblical response.

We must not separate the creation from its Creator; knowledge of God must come through both general revelation (nature) and special revelation (the Bible). The theologian Louis Berkhof said, "Since the entrance of sin into the world, man can gather true knowledge about God from His general revelation only if he studies it in the light of Scripture."[8] It is only then that the *entire* truth about God and what is seen around us can be fully understood and used to help people understand the bad news in Genesis and the good news of Jesus Christ.

---

[7] See D. Humphreys, *Starlight and Time* (Green Forest, AR: Master Books, 1994); and *The New Answers Book,* chapter 19 by Jason Lisle, (Green Forest, AR: Master Books, 2006), 245–254.

[8] L. Berkhof, Introductory volume to *Systematic Theology* (Grand Rapids, MI: Wm. B. Eerdmans Publ. Co., 1946), 60.

Index of Authors

Index of Scripture

15688376R10062

Made in the USA
Charleston, SC
15 November 2012